50 Ways to Save Our Children

Small, Medium, & Big Ways
You Can Change a Child's Life

by Cheryl Sab

Founder, www.50ways.org, and Executive Director of the Saban Children's Foundation

📘 HarperTrophy®

An Imprint of HarperCollins*Publishers*

*This book is lovingly dedicated
to children everywhere.*

Harper Trophy® is a registered trademark of
HarperCollins Publishers Inc.

50 Ways to Save Our Children
Copyright © 2002 by Cheryl Saban

Library of Congress Cataloging-in-Publication Data
Saban, Cheryl.
    50 ways to save our children : small, medium, & big ways you can change
a child's life / by Cheryl Saban.
        p. cm.
    ISBN 0-06-449038-6 (pbk.)
    1. Children—Services for—United States. 2. Children—Services for—United
States—Directories. 3. Child welfare—United States. 4. Voluntarism—United
States. I. Title: Fifty ways to save our children. II. Title.
HV741 .S2 2002   2001051455
362.7'0973—dc21   CIP
                                                                    AC

Typography by Henrietta Stern
❖
First Harper Trophy edition, 2002
Visit us on the World Wide Web!
www.harperchildrens.com

Contents

Part 3: Big Ways 83

50
Ways to
Save
Our Children

Introduction

When faced with a child in need, most people respond with compassion and generosity. Too often, however, many of us get lost somewhere between our good intentions and good deeds. It can be confusing and overwhelming to figure out what to do to make a difference.

50 Ways to Save Our Children helps well-meaning citizens navigate the maze of philanthropic possibilities. Hundreds of thousands of nonprofit agencies, clinics, coalitions, councils, leagues, projects, and other groups offer charitable assistance to needy children and their families. This book profiles a sampling of some leading organizations and activities that help to ease a broad spectrum of problems facing children today. Some of the charities listed here may be familiar to you; others may not be. Each has a proven track record of service to children.

The programs listed here really do make a difference, and by supporting them with your time and your financial resources, you can make a difference, too. As a volunteer, you join the ranks of Americans who give more than 2 billion hours each year to volunteer work. Giving of yourself allows you to see beyond the trials and challenges of your daily life; you will discover happiness not in what you have, but in what you give away.

Don't underestimate your importance; your efforts may be all that it takes to change the direction of a child's life. Sometimes people see so many problems in the world that they feel tempted to throw up their hands and quit trying to help, assuming that the efforts of one person couldn't possibly create meaningful change. But we can never know the many ways our simple acts of kindness affect the lives of others. Consider the starfish story:

> *One day a little girl was walking on the beach with her grandfather. It was low tide, and sprinkled along*

the shore as far as she could see were hundreds, maybe thousands of starfish. They were stranded on the sand, out of the water, helpless and dying in the heat of the sun. Every few steps, the little girl picked up a starfish and tossed it back into the sea. After walking this way for a while, the grandfather asked, "Why are you doing that, Mary? There are so many of them. You can't possibly save them all." The little girl stooped down, gingerly picked up another starfish, and tossed it into the sea. "But I saved that one, Grandpa."

What we do as individuals *does* make a difference. You can change the life of a child.

GOOD DEEDS ON THE INTERNET

The organizations listed in this book represent a tiny fraction of the volunteer and donation opportunities that exist in your community. You can learn more about activities in your area and research charities not listed here by using the Internet.

The following searchable websites help match volunteers with organizations that need help:

www.helping.org This website enables you to find volunteer and giving opportunities in your own community. It also helps you find a charity of your choice if you're interested in making a donation online. Since the AOL Time Warner Foundation underwrites the administrative costs of the site, 100 percent of your donation goes to the charity of your choice. If you have questions not answered on the website, call (703) 265-1342.

www.servenet.org All you have to do is enter your zip code, city, state, skills, and interests, and you will be matched with volunteer opportunities in your area. For more information, contact (202) 296-2992.

www.volunteermatch.org This site lists both onetime and ongoing
volunteer opportunities with nonprofit organizations in your
community. You can search by zip code, areas of interest, and date.
For more information, call (415) 241–6872 or (415) 241–6868.

You can use the Internet to research charitable organizations and the
way they use the donations they receive. The following sites can help:

www.give.org This is the website of the BBB Wise Giving Alliance,
which was formed by the merger of the National Charities Information
Bureau and the Council of Better Business Bureau's Philanthropic
Advisory Service. It provides information on national and international
charities. For more information, call (703) 276–0100.

www.guidestar.org This database includes information on more than
700,000 nonprofit organizations in the United States. You can obtain
information about a charity or philanthropic organization to decide
whether you would like to make a financial contribution. For more
information, call (757) 229–4631.

Part 1

Small Ways

"Small" does not mean unimportant.

The ideas for service presented in this

section are straightforward and simple,

but they can have a profound influence

on a child's life.

StandUp For Kids!

Every day thirteen runaway and homeless children die on the streets of the United States. Some are murdered, some die from disease, and others choose suicide as a way to end their lives of despair. Most of us never hear about these lost children, but they are not alone. According to the National Runaway Switchboard, there are at least 1.3 million runaway and homeless youth in the United States at any given time. The true figure is much higher since this number does not include children who are kicked out of their homes or become displaced from homeless families.

PARENTING TIP
Let your child know your love is unconditional.

Children end up on the street for a multitude of sad reasons. They are sometimes scared to go home to abuse, neglect, and violence from their parents or caretakers. Some kids get in trouble and try to escape the consequences of their choices. Some kids assume they can handle life on their own, but they face brutal, unforgiving situations on the street. Almost half of all runaway kids turn to prostitution within forty-eight hours of leaving home. Many sell drugs, steal, or beg to make enough money to eat.

Since 1990 StandUp For Kids and its national network of volunteers has been walking the streets to rescue and educate homeless and at-risk youth. Volunteers have discovered children in abandoned buildings, alleyways, dumpsters, and cardboard boxes. Often these children desperately need medical care; StandUp volunteers have found children with stab wounds, broken bones, infected bites and sores, and venereal diseases and AIDS.

StandUp For Kids lets these lost children know that someone cares. Volunteers have been trained to listen and to help children use the community resources available to meet their needs. StandUp For Kids sends counselors out to search for these children, guide them to shelters, give them food, and, hopefully, help them get off the street.

StandUp For Kids sponsors eighteen outreach programs in eight states, and they plan to expand by an additional twenty-five programs in the coming years. The program relies on volunteers; the group pays only three staff members: one part-time employee and two paid street kids who help train and work with volunteers. The program needs financial support, as well as hands-on help with administrative tasks in area offices.

You can make a free donation by purchasing a magazine subscription through *www.magazines.com* and choosing StandUp For Kids as the organization to receive a contribution. Barnes & Noble booksellers will contribute 5 percent of the cost of books you buy to the charity if you enter the Barnes & Noble website through the StandUp For Kids site.

For more information about getting involved, contact StandUp For Kids, P.O. Box 121, Chula Vista, CA 91912; call (800) 365–4KID; or visit the website *www.standupforkids.org*.

IF YOU CAN DO MORE: If you can make an ongoing commitment to homeless children, consider becoming a StandUp For Kids volunteer counselor. After about twenty hours of training, you will be ready to walk the streets at night, meeting and helping homeless and street kids. Most volunteers work three to four hours per week, and they work with and assist about twenty-five to thirty kids in a given month.

☙ WORDS OF WISDOM ❧

"If you put a little on a little, soon it will become a lot."
—HESIOD (ANCIENT POET)

Use Your Computer to Make Free Online Donations

If you have access to a computer, you can earn donations for your favorite charities without spending a penny. A growing number of websites have click-to-donate features so that advertisers make a donation every time you use the site or view an advertisement. Other websites allow you to shop online and dedicate a percentage of your purchase amount to the charity of your choice.

One of the leading charity shopping websites, *iGive.com*, directs up to 33 percent of each purchase to the charity of your choice. (The exact amount depends on the company's arrangement with the merchant.) This is an easy and painless way to donate. You simply shop in the convenience of your own home for items you were planning to buy anyway. This simple gesture has raised hundreds of thousands of dollars for various charities. The site has earned the Good Housekeeping Web Site Certification for privacy, quality, and efficiency. In addition, the website generates a Tax-Deduction Report so you can keep track of your donations for the year, as well as a Shopping Activity Report, which itemizes your purchases and the causes they benefited.

PARENTING TIP
Spend one-on-one time with your child every day.

You can also make free contributions by using the Internet search engine *www.searchtohelp.com* and other charity search engines. When you visit the site, search the web with the search box, click on sponsors' banners, or send free e-cards, various sponsors make donations to charity. Each action earns a few pennies, but they add up fast. If you were to visit the site once a day and make one search and click on two advertisement banners, you would earn about ten dollars a month for charity. The charities receiving the funds are chosen monthly by a user poll.

Many other e-philanthropy charitable donation sites have sprung up as well. Give these a look:

www.4goodnesssake.org You can choose from dozens of charities to receive credit at this click-to-donate site.

www.aidforteens.com This site raises money for charities that work with teens in need; funds are raised through searches, viewing ads, and shopping online.

www.charityCafe.com This search-and-donate site includes GoTo, YellowPages, and Ask Jeeves, among other search engines.

www.charity-frog.com This click-to-donate site credits the American Red Cross.

www.donate4free.org This click-to-donate site raises funds for Save the Children and The Hunger Site, among others.

www.donationjunction.com This click-to-donate site benefits charities dealing with children, hunger, land mines, and the environment, among others.

www.endcancernow.com This click-to-donate site raises funds for the American Cancer Society.

www.endhomelessnessnow.com This click-to-donate site benefits the homeless; the site will send an e-mail to registered participants to remind them to donate daily.

www.feedahungrychild.com Click on the cup to donate a cup of free food to hungry children in Honduras or Haiti.

www.freedonation.com This click-to-donate site benefits charities supporting children, food aid, education, and the environment, among other causes.

www.hitsagainsthunger.com When you click on the dollar bill and drag it to HungerPig, the pig grunts and a dollar is donated to fight hunger. (You can donate once a day.)

www.iGive.com Enter various shopping websites through this site and stores in the e-mall will donate a percentage of your sale to the charity of your choice. More than 230 stores participate, including Toys R Us, Amazon.com, Lands' End, and Wal-Mart.

www.quickdonations.com This click-to-donate site includes many charities dealing with hunger.

www.thecharitypot.com This site allows you to donate to charity through shopping and using sponsoring Internet search engines.

www.thehungersite.com This click-to-donate and shop-to-donate site helps fight hunger.

www.wedid.net This click-to-donate site assists charities that work on autism, cancer, diabetes, and mental health issues, among others.

IF YOU CAN DO MORE: Rather than periodically visit these sites, you could use them on a regular basis. For example, you could visit a click-to-donate site every time you open your e-mail. You could also share these websites with your friends so that they can make free donations as well.

❧ *WORDS OF WISDOM* ❧

"In optimistic moments, I like to believe that most Americans would want to lift children out of poverty even if it costs something."

—Dr. Laura D'Andrea Tyson,
former chair, President's Council of
Economic Advisors

The 3 United Way

Charity begins at home, and for the United Way that means in your hometown. The United Way system includes nearly two thousand community-based United Way organizations, each governed by local volunteers. Through a single community-wide campaign, United Way volunteers raise funds to support local nonprofit charities. The umbrella group then shares and distributes funds to participating groups in your community.

~
PARENTING TIP
Monitor your child's television viewing. Watch with him and discuss what you see.
~

United Way contributes funds to a wide range of organizations, including those dedicated to youth development, crisis intervention, disaster relief, and emergency shelter, among many others. Every group receiving United Way funds must be a nonprofit, tax-exempt charity governed by volunteers; it must provide services at reasonable cost; and it must have a policy of nondiscrimination.

For more information, contact The United Way at 701 North Fairfax Street, Alexandria, VA 22314–2045; call (703) 836–7111; or visit the website *www.unitedway.org*. To find the United Way organization nearest you, enter your zip code on the Local United Way search box on the main website.

IF YOU CAN DO MORE: Rather than simply making a personal donation, consider coordinating a United Way fund drive in your office, church, or school.

"Everybody can be great because anybody can serve."

—DR. MARTIN LUTHER KING, JR.

Doctors Without Borders

Doctors Without Borders is an international relief organization that provides emergency medical care to people in crisis—including many children—throughout the world. This organization aids victims of armed conflict, epidemics, and natural and man-made disasters; it also helps others who lack health care due to geographic remoteness.

The organization was founded in 1971 by a group of French doctors who believed that all people have the right to medical care and that this need supersedes respect for national borders. Annually more than two thousand volunteers work in more than eighty countries in front-line hospitals, refugee camps, disaster sites, towns, and villages.

PARENTING TIP

Remember that laughter is a great healer.

In addition to giving medical care, the volunteers bear witness and speak out against the underlying causes of suffering and bring the concerns of their patients to public forums. For example, volunteers with Doctors Without Borders have spoken out against the atrocities they have witnessed in Chechnya, Angola, and Kosovo, among other places.

The organization relies on donations from individuals, foundations, governments, and international agencies. A donation of $35 can provide medical, sanitation, and logistical material to save one cholera patient. A gift of $100 can provide vaccinations against meningitis, measles, or polio for a hundred people .

For more information, contact the Doctors Without Borders U.S. headquarters at 6 East 39th Street, 8th Floor,

New York, NY 10016; or call (888) 392–0392 or (212) 679–6800. You can also visit the website *www.doctorswith-outborders.org.*

IF YOU CAN DO MORE: If you have medical training and would like to volunteer, contact the New York office for an interview. Most volunteers work for six months to one year, although general surgeons and anesthesiologists with experience may be accepted for shorter assignments. If you aren't a medical professional but want to help out, the group is always looking for volunteers to assist with administrative and clerical work in the office.

❧ *WORDS OF WISDOM* ❧
"How will each of us add to or subtract from
America's moral bank account when the God
of the universe asks for an accounting?"

—MARIAN WRIGHT EDELMAN,
CHILDREN'S DEFENSE FUND

5 Goodwill Industries

Goodwill Industries has proven that the power of work can transform lives. Work builds self-confidence, independence, and competence—all traits that help parents provide stable and healthy environments for their children. Sometimes, in order to help the children, you must help their parents first.

~
PARENTING TIP
Praise and smiles make a difference. Catch your kids being good.
~

Goodwill Industries provides people with the tools they need to succeed in working. The organization is one of the world's largest non-profit providers of employment and training services for people with disabilities and other problems such as welfare, homelessness, and illiteracy.

Goodwill Industries's 181 local, autonomous member organizations in the United States and Canada provide job training and employment programs, job placement opportunities, and postemployment support to help people become independent, tax-paying members of their communities.

There are many ways to help Goodwill Industries, from donating old clothing, computers, and household goods, to shopping at any of the more than 1,700 stores in North America or on the website *www.shopgoodwill.com*. Retail sales of donated goods account for about half the organization's revenue. The money spent in Goodwill stores goes to support job training and placement programs for people with disabilities and other disadvantages.

To find out more about Goodwill, contact Goodwill Industries International, Inc., 9200 Rockville Pike,

Bethesda, MD 20814; call (800) 664–6577; or visit the website *www.goodwill.org.*

IF YOU CAN DO MORE: If you are in a position to hire an employee, consider a candidate from Goodwill. Goodwill Industries provides training in computer programming, health care, financial services, and hospitality, among other skills. By hiring someone trained by Goodwill, you and your company are giving the candidate a chance to develop invaluable work experience, which can be used to generate additional work.

❦ *WORDS OF WISDOM* ❦

"Ultimately a great nation is a compassionate nation. No individual or nation can be great if it does not have a concern for 'the least of these.'"

—Dr. Martin Luther King, Jr.

6
American Red Cross

The American Red Cross is a humanitarian organization led by more than one million volunteers who strive to save lives and ease suffering in its many forms. Volunteers provide relief to victims of disasters and emergencies, collect half the nation's blood supply, and teach first aid and CPR courses, among many other activities. In the wake of an earthquake, tornado, flood, fire, hurricane, or other disaster, the Red Cross is there.

PARENTING TIP
Help your child develop self-esteem by providing lots of positive feedback.

The Red Cross works locally, nationally, and internationally. The group is independent, politically neutral, and nondiscriminatory. To find the Red Cross chapter nearest you, use the website to search by zip code.

You can also give the gift of life by donating blood to the Red Cross. A single donation of blood can help save up to three lives. Donating blood is safe, easy, and convenient. Donors may give blood at blood drives conducted at high schools, colleges, churches, companies, and community organizations. Red Cross donor centers also accept donations. The donation process takes only about one hour.

The Red Cross also coordinates a tissue donation service. A single tissue donor can potentially benefit as many as fifty people. In fact, more than 600,000 lives have been saved or enhanced since the establishment of the American Red Cross Tissue Services in 1982. All you have to do is sign a donor card or driver's license and let your family know about your wishes (next of kin is asked for consent).

To find out about donating blood, call (800) GIVE–LIFE. To learn about tissue donation, call (888) 4–TISSUE. To make a donation by phone, call (800) HELP–NOW. If you want to make a contribution to your local Red Cross chapter, please mention the Local Community Services Fund when calling in the donation. To donate to the disaster relief operation, mention the Disaster Relief Fund when making the donation. Finally, to make a donation to an international crisis, mention the International Response Fund when making your donation. You may also visit the website *www.redcross.org.*

IF YOU CAN DO MORE: If you would like to volunteer, you should contact your local chapter for more information about how to get involved in your community. (Most international disaster relief workers have extensive specialized training.) Consider arranging a blood drive in your place of work or school. Even making the effort to go with a friend or two to donate blood a few times a year could make a huge difference in someone's life.

༜ *WORDS OF WISDOM* ༜

"We need to treat our children as the most precious commodity on the planet."

—Dr. Ronald S. Cohen,
executive director, United Cerebral
Palsy of Los Angeles

Donate Books to Your Local Grammar School

Books bring pleasure to children. They can be read and enjoyed countless times, opening a world of imagination and creativity to children of all ages. Unfortunately, books are scarce in too many communities and schools.

↪

PARENTING TIP
Celebrate your child's achievements— even the small ones.

↪

Take a minute to look through your bookshelf and pull out a few books in good condition that your children have outgrown. Most public schools need additional books for their libraries or classroom collections and welcome donations. You could also ask the school what books they need and buy books to donate. Many children's hospitals and shelters also need books.

IF YOU CAN DO MORE: Consider coordinating a book drive by soliciting books or donations from others in your community. As part of the campaign, you could arrange to have a book plate placed in every donated book that read "This book was donated in honor of . . ." For more information on organizing a book drive, contact *www.booksforkids.org*, an organization that promotes literacy among at-risk kids in Washington State.

If you're interested in providing books overseas, consider making a donation to the International Book Bank (*www.internationalbookbank.org*) or Book Aid International (*www.bookaid.org*), both of which provide books and educational materials to needy countries.

*"If a free society cannot help the many who are poor,
it cannot save the few who are rich."*

—JOHN F. KENNEDY, INAUGURAL ADDRESS,
JANUARY 20, 1961

Easter Seals

One out of every five Americans has a disability, and Easter Seals is there to offer them help and hope. Each year Easter Seals helps more than one million children and adults with disabilities gain greater independence and achieve their goals.

Nationwide as many as 54 million Americans have a disability. Who are these people? The child with cerebral palsy, the neighbor injured in a car accident, the grandmother recovering from a stroke. Easter Seals children's services help kids with disabilities succeed in school. Easter Seals employment programs help people learn job skills and enter the workplace. Easter Seals medical rehabilitation services help people return to their everyday lives after suffering from spinal cord injuries, stroke, polio, and other disabling events.

PARENTING TIP
Share a cuddle and a giggle with your children every day.

Easter Seals provides early intervention programs for children with disabilities, to help them adapt and find ways to succeed in school and in their lives. Easter Seals was the first national voluntary agency to speak and act on behalf of children with disabilities in the 1920s.

For more information, contact Easter Seals at 230 West Monroe Street, Suite 1800, Chicago, IL 60606; call (800) 221–6827; or visit the website *www.easter-seals.org*.

IF YOU CAN DO MORE: Easter Seals always needs volunteers to help with office work, to work at special events and camps, and to work with children and families in need. If you think you can make an ongoing effort, contact the national office for a referral to your local Easter Seals chapter.

∾ *WORDS OF WISDOM* ∾

"We have but one life. We get nothing out
of that life except by putting something into it. To relieve
suffering, to help the unfortunate, to do kind acts and deeds
is, after all, the one sure way to secure happiness or to
achieve real success. Your life and mine shall be valued not
by what we take . . . but by what we give."

—Edgar Allen, founder, Easter Seals

9 Futures for Children

Futures for Children works on American Indian reservations where the school drop-out rate is highest, the employment rate is lowest, health care is the worst in the nation, and opportunities for children seem remote. The group teaches self-help skills and community development strategies in Hopi, Navajo, and Pueblo tribal communities of the Southwest.

In addition, Futures for Children sponsors a mentoring program that helps American Indian students succeed in school. (On many American Indian reservations, only half of the students entering first grade will finish high school.) As part of the Friendship Program, a sponsor is paired with a specific American Indian child; the sponsor corresponds with the child and provides financial help to the child's family. A $420 yearly gift helps pay for school supplies and books, as well as youth leadership training and community education programs.

PARENTING TIP
Remember
what it was like
to be a child.

To find out how you can help, contact Futures for Children, 9600 Tennyson Street, NE, Albuquerque, NM 87122; call (800) 545–6843; or visit the website *www.futuresforchildren.org.*

IF YOU CAN DO MORE: You can coordinate a sponsor recruitment gathering at your office or in your community to encourage a group of people to work together in sponsoring children. You could also purchase jewelry and clothing from Futures for Children to help raise funds.

"*The test of our progress is not whether we add more to the abundance of those who have much; it is whether we provide enough for those who have too little.*"

—FRANKLIN DELANO ROOSEVELT

ChildSight

It is estimated that approximately 25 percent, or 1.8 million, of all secondary students living in poverty in America cannot see clearly what is written on their classroom blackboards. The cause is often refractive error, or the inability to see near or at a distance. These problems frequently go undetected among impoverished children who do not have access to proper health care.

Fortunately, 95 percent of the problems associated with refractive error can be treated with eyeglasses. ChildSight identifies and treats the nation's poor children suffering from this problem. ChildSight is a unique school-based vision screening and eyeglass distribution program that works to improve the vision—and the educational performance—of poor secondary school students.

PARENTING TIP

Make eye contact when you speak with your child.

Children cannot learn in the traditional way if they cannot see. Without the ability to see clearly, a child cannot read the blackboard, use the periodic table, dissect a frog, or read an overhead projector. In New Jersey, 90 percent of teachers surveyed whose students received eyeglasses from ChildSight noticed an improvement in students' class participation.

For more information or to make a donation, contact ChildSight at 90 West Street, Suite 200, New York, NY 10006; call (212) 766–5266; or visit the website *www.childsight.org.*

IF YOU CAN DO MORE: ChildSight currently

serves children in fourteen cities in the United States. If the program is not available in your school system, consider coordinating an effort to bring the program to a needy community in your area. The program needs the support of the local school board, in addition to the dedication of principals, teachers, and school health services.

☙ *WORDS OF WISDOM* ☙

"Life is an exciting business and most exciting when it is lived for others."

—HELEN KELLER

Make-A-Wish Foundation

Share the power of a wish! Make-A-Wish Foundation grants wishes to thousands of children with life-threatening illnesses each year. Since it was founded in 1980, the Make-A-Wish Foundation has granted a wish to every qualified child referred to them—more than 83,000 wishes to children worldwide.

The Make-A-Wish Foundation becomes aware of a child's wish through wish referrals sent by parents, guardians, doctors, nurses, and social workers. Most wishes fall under one of four categories: "I want to have . . . ," "I want to go . . . ," "I want to be . . . ," or "I want to meet. . . ." Every effort is made to make every child's wish come true.

PARENTING TIP

Love your spouse; your children can sense it.

Wish granting can be costly, and your financial support is appreciated. In addition to offering financial aid, you can also help the Make-A-Wish Foundation by donating your frequent flyer miles and hotel loyalty points. These contributions enable the foundation to send thousands of seriously ill children and their families on the trip of a lifetime.

To find out more about how you can help, contact Make-A-Wish Foundation of America, 3550 North Central Avenue, Suite 300, Phoenix, AZ 85012; call (800) 722–WISH; or visit the website *www.makeawish.org*.

IF YOU CAN DO MORE: You can join more than twenty thousand volunteers worldwide who work to help make children's wishes come true. The

Make-A-Wish Foundation of America is always looking for volunteers in wish granting, development and fundraising, medical outreach, public relations, and special events. Contact the national office for a referral to one of the eighty-one chapters nationwide.

❧ WORDS OF WISDOM ❧

"I don't know what your destiny will be, but one thing I know: the only ones among you who will be really happy are those who have sought and found how to serve."

—ALBERT SCHWEITZER

National Mental Health Association

One out of every five children has a diagnosable mental, emotional, or behavioral disorder, and as many as one out of every ten may suffer from a serious emotional disturbance. Despite these high figures, 70 percent of children do not receive mental health services. The National Mental Health Association wants to turn those numbers around.

The National Mental Health Association is the country's oldest and largest nonprofit mental health organization. It works to improve the mental health of all Americans, especially the 54 million individuals with mental disorders, by educating people about mental illness and reducing barriers to treatment and services. The association is unique in that it is the only national nonprofit organization that addresses all aspects of mental health and mental illness.

PARENTING TIP
Find a common interest with your child.

The association was established in 1909 by a former psychiatric patient who was subjected to horrible abuse during the time he spent in various public and private institutions. His reform efforts eventually took shape as the National Mental Health Association.

For more information, contact the National Mental Health Association, 1021 Prince Street, Alexandria, VA 22314; call (800) 969–NMHA or (703) 684–7722; or visit the website *www.nmha.org*.

IF YOU CAN DO MORE: The National Mental Health Association works with more than 340 affiliates nationwide. If you can make an ongoing effort to support mental health issues in your community, contact the national office for a referral to an agency in your area.

WARNING SIGNS

If you see any warning signs of mental illness in your child or a child you know, it is important to seek help from a mental health professional. Treating a mental health problem in childhood can prevent more serious problems later in life. Seek help if a child:

- feels very sad or hopeless
- feels overly anxious or worried
- experiences excessive irritability
- is unduly scared or fearful
- has frequent nightmares
- experiences excessive or misdirected anger
- uses alcohol or drugs
- wants to be alone all of the time
- hears voices or has visions
- has trouble sitting still, concentrating, or focusing
- needs to wash his or her hands, count his or her steps, check appliances or plugs, or perform other rituals repeatedly
- talks about suicide or death
- hurts animals
- damages property
- fights with or injures other people
- has major changes in sleeping habits
- has major changes in eating habits
- loses interest in friends or schoolwork
- experiences a drop in academic performance

Encourage your child to talk about his or her emotions, and don't be afraid to seek appropriate help if needed.

LEADING CHILDREN'S MENTAL HEALTH WEBSITES

www.aacap.org American Academy of Child and Adolescent Psychiatry

www.psych.org American Psychiatric Association

www.apa.org American Psychological Association

www.ffcmh.org Federation of Families for Children's Mental Health

www.hskids-tmsc.org Head Start Mental Health Resources

www.mentalhealth.org Knowledge Exchange Network

www.sshsac.org Safe Schools/Healthy Students Action Center

❧ WORDS OF WISDOM ❧

"Teach us to give and not to count the cost."

—IGNATIUS LOYOLA

Muscular Dystrophy Association

There are no incurable diseases, only diseases for which no treatments have yet been found—that is the basic philosophy of the Muscular Dystrophy Association, a voluntary national health agency dedicated to conquering neuromuscular diseases, which affect more than one million American children and adults.

The Muscular Dystrophy Association supports nearly 400 research projects worldwide, and it operates more than 200 offices and 230 hospital-affiliated clinics. People affected by any of the disorders in MDA's program have access to a nationwide network of clinics staffed by top health professionals. MDA also provides summer camps for children ages six to twenty-one geared to the special needs of campers with neuromuscular diseases. These programs are funded almost entirely by individual private contributors; MDA collects no fees from those it serves.

PARENTING TIP

Ask your children to help you; they want to be needed.

MDA supports more research on neuromuscular diseases than any other private-sector organization in the world. MDA scientists are in the forefront of gene therapy research and have uncovered the genetic defects responsible for several forms of muscular dystrophy.

MDA raises funds through the annual Jerry Lewis MDA Telethon on Labor Day weekend. Other fundraisers—bowling tournaments, golf tournaments, and walk-a-thons, among others—take place year-round.

There are many ways to help, including volunteering

and donating. For more information, contact Muscular Dystrophy Association, National Headquarters, 3300 East Sunrise Drive, Tucson, AZ 85718; call (800) 572–1717; or visit the website *www.mdausa.org.*

IF YOU CAN DO MORE: Two million volunteers work with MDA programs, helping with summer camp, support groups, seminars, telethons, and other special events. You might consider supporting one of these activities or coordinating a local fundraiser for MDA.

🌿 *WORDS OF WISDOM* 🌿
"Goodness is the only investment that never fails."

—HENRY DAVID THOREAU, *WALDEN*

14 Hole in the Wall Gang Camp

Each summer the Hole in the Wall Gang Camp provides love, hope, and unbridled joy to a thousand seriously ill children who have cancer, sickle-cell anemia, HIV/AIDS, and other serious diseases. The camp, tucked in the northeastern Connecticut woods, offers fishing, swimming, arts and crafts, horseback riding, and other activities. It also provides around-the-clock medical supervision with doctors, nurses, and many training volunteers.

∽

PARENTING TIP
Make yourself
available.

∽

The Wall Gang Camp has year-round programs to continue to provide "the experience of a lifetime" to children and their families who face devastating health challenges. The camp provides free programs for health care professionals and teachers, reunions for campers, and bereavement weekends.

The seed money for the Hole in the Wall Gang Camp was made possible through Paul Newman's profits from Newman's Own, but the camp now stands on its own. The camp compiles a wish list of things it needs each year, including inexpensive items such as art supplies, film, and board games, as well as more costly things such as playground equipment, computers, and industrial vacuum cleaners.

For more information, contact the Hole in the Wall Gang Fund at 555 Long Wharf Drive, New Haven, CT 06511; call (203) 772–0522; or visit the website *www.holeinthewallgang.org.*

IF YOU CAN DO MORE: Volunteers are needed

each summer to assist with the campers and to keep the program running smoothly.

❧ WORDS OF WISDOM ❧

*"Where I was born and where and how
I have lived is unimportant. It is what I have done with
where I have been that should be of interest."*

—Georgia O'Keeffe

15 Prevent Child Abuse America

The number of children abused or neglected is, sadly, a staggering figure. A major study conducted in 1993 using a "harm standard" revealed an estimated 3 million abused and neglected children in the United States alone. Three children each day die from abuse or neglect.

Something must be done to protect these helpless citizens, and Prevent Child Abuse America is leading the way. The organization was founded on the belief that everyone has a responsibility to help provide the nation's children with a safe and nurturing environment in which to grow. The group achieves this goal by promoting legislation, policies, and programs that help to prevent child abuse and neglect, support healthy childhood development, and strengthen families. Prevent Child Abuse America works on local and state issues through its network of forty-one state chapters and local affiliates. The group also works on the national level as an active member of the National Child Abuse Coalition, a group of more than thirty professional child advocacy organizations.

> **PARENTING TIP**
> Respect your
> children.

Prevent Child Abuse America sponsors the Healthy Families America program (a national program to help parents of newborns get their children off to a healthy start), the National Center on Child Abuse Prevention Research, and Self-Help Parent Support Programs (confidential weekly meetings free to parents interested in strengthening their parenting skills), among other programs.

For more information or to make a donation, contact

Prevent Child Abuse America, 200 South Michigan Avenue, 17th Floor, Chicago, IL 60604; call (312) 663–3520 or (800) 555–3748; or visit the website *www.preventchildabuse.org*.

IF YOU CAN DO MORE: Consider working with a Prevent Child Abuse America affiliate in your area to create a public awareness campaign in your community. Studies have found that one-third of all Americans have seen an adult physically abuse a child and two-thirds have witnessed an adult emotionally abuse a child. Public awareness of the problem is an important step toward stopping this abuse.

✈ *WORDS OF WISDOM*✈
"He has half the deed done who
has made a beginning."

—HORACE

16 Child Welfare League of America

Every child deserves a loving, stable, and protective home. Most families want to provide for their children and do a good job. But sometimes families and kids need guidance. That's when the Child Welfare League of America can help.

The Child Welfare League of America promotes the well-being of children and strives to protect every child from harm. The league is an umbrella organization of more than a thousand agencies in fifty states and the District of Columbia that provide direct services to children and their families. The league conducts hundreds of conferences and seminars on child welfare each year; it advocates for legislation to support children; it trains child day-care providers to train parents about positive parenting. The league also sponsors the Protecting America's Children: It's Everybody's Business campaign, an initiative to stop child abuse and neglect.

PARENTING TIP
Help your children learn something new.

The Child Welfare League of America was founded when President Teddy Roosevelt held the first White House meeting on children in 1909. At that time one of the central issues involved child labor and the challenges facing children who worked in factories at very low wages to help support their families. Today the league and its member agencies work on issues such as adoption, foster care, child care, homelessness, drug abuse, and HIV infection, among others.

The Child Welfare League supports its member agencies through leadership, research, publications, and advocacy. The group also works to educate the American public about the needs of abused and neglected children. The league develops standards for service in areas such as child protection, foster care, adoption, and child care.

For more information or to make a donation, contact the Child Welfare League of America, 440 First Street, N.W., 3rd Floor, Washington, DC 20001; call (202) 638–2952; or visit the website *www.cwla.org*.

> **IF YOU CAN DO MORE:** The Child Welfare League of America believes that protecting America's children is everybody's responsibility. Contact the league for information about member agencies and activities in your area. Child abuse does happen in your neighborhood, and you can help to stop it.

❧ *WORDS OF WISDOM* ❧
"The reward of a thing well done, is to have done it."

—RALPH WALDO EMERSON

17
United Cerebral Palsy

It is estimated that some 500,000 children and adults in the United States suffer from cerebral palsy, a term used to describe a group of chronic disorders that appear in the first few years of life and inhibit control of movement. Identification of infants with cerebral palsy very early in life and early treatment can give them the best opportunity for developing to their full potential. United Cerebral Palsy, or UCP, is committed to making a difference for children and adults afflicted with these disorders. UCP is also one of the leading sources of information on cerebral palsy and a pivotal advocate for people with disabilities.

~
PARENTING TIP
Accept your
children as
they are.
~

UCP and its nationwide network of 114 affiliates work to ensure the inclusion of persons with disabilities in every facet of society. The group strives to advance the independence, productivity, and full citizenship of people with cerebral palsy and other disabilities. (Fully 65 percent of people served by UCP have disabilities other than cerebral palsy.) Every day, UCP affiliates serve more than 30,000 children and adults with disabilities through programs such as physical therapy, early intervention, family support, social and recreational programs, state and local referrals, employment assistance, and advocacy.

About 5,000 babies are diagnosed with the condition each year. Cerebral palsy is caused by damage to one or more specific areas of the brain, usually occurring during fetal development; before, during, or shortly after birth; or during infancy. Risk factors include premature birth, low birth weight, Rh or A-B-O blood type incompatibility between mother and infant, infection by the mother with German measles or other viruses during pregnancy, bacterial infection, or prolonged loss of oxygen during the birthing process. Some cases involve head injury during the first two years of life.

UCP also sponsors the UCP Research and Education Foundation, the nation's principal nongovernment agency sponsoring research on the prevention of cerebral palsy and the improvement of quality of life of people with disabilities. The foundation has been instrumental in eliminating two of the major causes of cerebral palsy, German measles and maternal-child blood type incompatibility.

For more information, contact United Cerebral Palsy Association, Inc., 1660 L Street, N.W., Suite 700, Washington, DC 20036; call (800) 872–5827; or visit the website *www.4mychild.*

> **IF YOU CAN DO MORE:** If there is no UCP office in your area, you may want to organize a local affiliate. UCP works closely with its affiliates on issues, so you won't need to go it alone. You can help to provide a strong voice for children and adults with disabilities and their families. For more information on starting an affiliate, call UPC Affiliate Services at (800) 872–5827.

❧ WORDS OF WISDOM ❧

"Whatever you can do or dream you can, begin it. Boldness has genius, power, and magic in it. Begin it now."

—GOETHE

18 Children's Defense Fund

Founded in 1973, the mission of the Children's Defense Fund is to leave no child behind and to ensure every child a healthy start, a head start, a fair start, a safe start, and a moral start in life and successful passage to adulthood, with the help of caring families and communities.

↩
PARENTING TIP
Have patience with your children.
↩

CDF provides a strong, effective voice for all children of America who cannot vote, lobby, or speak for themselves. The group is mindful of the needs of all children, but pays particular attention to the needs of poor and minority children and those with disabilities. CDF educates the nation about the needs of children and encourages prevention before they get sick, drop out of school, or get in trouble.

For more information, contact the Children's Defense Fund, 25 E Street, N.W., Washington, DC 20001; call (202) 628–8787; or visit the website *www.childrensdefense.org.*

IF YOU CAN DO MORE: CDF offers a variety of projects that individuals or organizations can implement at the local level. CDF provides training and ongoing technical support for many projects. The projects include the Community Monitoring Project (which examines the impact of welfare changes on children in specific communities), Freedom Schools (summer programs for children who have no other options), and the Child Health Implementation Project (which works to spread the word about free and low-cost health insurance for children), among others.

---

10 KEY FACTS ABOUT AMERICAN CHILDREN

1 in 2 will live in a single-parent family at some point in childhood.

1 in 7 has no health insurance.

1 in 7 has a worker in their family but still is poor.

1 in 8 never graduates from high school.

1 in 8 is born to a teenage mother.

1 in 12 has a disability.

1 in 13 was born with low birth weight.

1 in 26 is born to a mother who received late or no prenatal care.

1 in 139 will die before reaching age 1.

1 in 1,056 will be killed by guns before age 20.

All data compiled by the Children's Defense Fund, *The State of America's Children Yearbook 2000*

❧ WORDS OF WISDOM ❧
"What's done to children, they will do to society."

—KARL MENNINGER

Children's Miracle Network

Children's Miracle Network is an international nonprofit organization dedicated to helping children by raising funds and awareness for 170 children's hospitals throughout North America. Each year these nonprofit hospitals treat more than 14 million children afflicted with diseases, injuries, and birth defects of every kind. They treat all children, regardless of affliction or the families' ability to pay. They are truly miracle workers.

PARENTING TIP
Respect your children's choices.

Since 1983 Children's Miracle Network has raised nearly $1.8 billion for children's hospitals—$1 at a time—through the sale of balloon tags sold at sponsoring retailers. Unlike many other charities, Children's Miracle Network allocates 100 percent of donations to the community where the funds are raised.

For more information or to find a corporate sponsor near you, contact Children's Miracle Network, 4525 South 2300 East, Salt Lake City, UT 84117; call (801) 278–8900; or visit the website *www.cmn.org*.

IF YOU CAN DO MORE: In addition to donating dollars, you can get involved with volunteer work at the hospitals sponsored by Children's Miracle Network. There are lots of ways to help: volunteer in the gift shop, learn to be a "cuddler" for babies who need extra attention, or donate blood. Sadly, children's hospitals always need it.

"*Never doubt that a small group of thoughtful, committed citizens can change the world; indeed, it's the only thing that ever has.*"

—Margaret Mead

20 SOS Children's Villages

There are more than a half million abused and/or neglected children in foster care systems in the United States. For some of these kids, traditional foster care works well, but not for all of them. Some kids stay in a kind of foster care limbo for years, moving from one home to another, with no chance to bond or form attachments. Too often siblings are separated from one another, never knowing whom to call family.

↩

PARENTING TIP

Listen to
the stories your
children tell.

↩

SOS Children's Villages offers an alternative for children in foster care: a permanent family and a home of their own. Every effort is made to keep brothers and sisters together. Each SOS Village is made up of about ten families that form communities where the children heal, grow, learn, and participate in neighborhood life. They leave the villages as young adults, equipped with a good education, motivation, and the strength of a stable, supportive family—in other words, with a firm foundation for leading independent, fulfilling lives.

SOS Children's Villages currently sponsors two villages in the United States—one in Florida north of Miami and a second in Illinois just outside Chicago—as well as villages in other countries. Some of the foster parents have grown children; others have never had children of their own. A state family court judge usually determines which children will be placed in SOS Children's Villages.

If you can help, contact SOS Children's Villages—USA, 1317 F Street, N.W., Suite 550, Washington, DC 20004; call (202) 347–7920; or visit the website *www.soschildrensvil-*

lages.org.

IF YOU CAN DO MORE: If you can commit to make regular donations, consider sponsoring a child at one of the international villages. If you think you have the special skills to devote yourself to loving and providing a stable home to foster children, consider being trained as an SOS parent.

❧ *WORDS OF WISDOM* ❧

"When children know uniqueness is respected, they are more likely to put theirs to use."

—Dorothy Corkille Briggs

Part 2

Medium Ways

You may be able to share more than your financial resources; you may be able to give time or talents on an ongoing basis. These suggestions show you how to share a little bit more.

Collect Toys and School Supplies for Homeless Shelters

Homelessness is a devastating experience for families. It disrupts almost every aspect of family life, interfering with children's education, shattering emotional health, and often resulting in the separation of family members.

One of the fastest-growing segments of the homeless population is families with children. Children account for 25 percent of the homeless, and half of them are under the age of five.

Homelessness can have dire consequences for children. Compared with housed poor children, homeless children experience worse health, more developmental delays, more anxiety and behavior problems, and lower performance in school. Homeless children don't enjoy the luxury of toys to call their own. You can help to bring joy to these children by remembering them with gifts throughout the year, not just at holiday time.

PARENTING TIP

Give your child the opportunity to explore the world.

Make a date on your calendar every year to collect toys and school supplies to donate to your local emergency or homeless shelter.

You can call your local department of children's and family services to locate a shelter near you. You can also look on the Internet; the websites discussed in the box in the introduction can help. In addition, consider contacting the National Coalition for the Homeless, 1012 Fourteenth Street, N.W., Suite 600, Washington, DC 20005–3471; call (202) 737–6444; or visit the website *www.nationalhomeless.org*.

IF YOU CAN DO MORE: Ask family, friends, and coworkers to make donations, too. In addition to items for children, shelters need clothes, toiletries, and household items. You might also consider volunteering at a homeless shelter. You can work behind the scenes answering phones, washing dishes, or doing administrative tasks; or you could work with children by organizing field trips or recreational activities. Contact your local shelter and find out what needs to be done. If you want to make a difference in a single family's situation, you may want to make a commitment to support a homeless family as they move out of the shelter and into a new home; you could contribute household goods, babysitting, and, of course, moral support.

A LOOK AND A SMILE

Many people ask the National Coalition for the Homeless about what to do when they encounter a homeless person asking for money. The decision about whether or not to give money is an individual, personal decision. However, many people on the street—those who are asking for money and those who are not—are often passed by countless times as though they did not exist. Acknowledging a person's existence by looking at them is one of the most important ways to reaffirm his or her humanity at a time when homelessness seems to have stripped it away. Whether or not you choose to give money, please don't look away as if the person doesn't exist.

"*Children are the supreme test of our
moral vision. They are because they are so vulnerable.
In a sense they stand as a crystallization, as an example, as a
kind of eternal symbol of our responsibility for each other,
since they are so dependent on us.*"

—FATHER BRYAN HEHIR,
HARVARD DIVINITY SCHOOL

22 Tuesday's Child

Tuesday's Child is a nonprofit organization that is passionately committed to meeting the material and emotional needs of families with children diagnosed with HIV infection or AIDS.

This organization strives to provide family-oriented services that ease the hardships these children and their families have to bear. Tuesday's Child endeavors to help families remain intact by providing both material assistance and emotional support to people living with HIV and AIDS. The Necessities Assistance Program delivers monthly supplies of diapers, formulas, and other goods for children under age three. The consistent monthly provision of baby food and formula plays a primary role in sparing HIV-positive mothers the choice between denying their babies nourishment and risking infection. A recent study conducted by the University of North Carolina linked stress to accelerated HIV disease progression among patients without symptoms; every increase in severe stress doubled the risk progression to AIDS. Tuesday's Child tries to minimize stress in the lives of HIV-positive mothers and their children.

> **PARENTING TIP**
> Listen to your child with your full attention.

The Family Service Program provides monthly opportunities for family recreational activities. Tuesday's Child also provides financial support for burial expenses.

To find out more about Tuesday's Child, contact the organization at Tuesday's Child, 8501 West Washington Boulevard, Culver City, CA 90232; call (310) 204–3848; or visit the website *www.pediatricaids.com*.

IF YOU CAN DO MORE: Your monetary donations make a difference: $25 will provide a child with diapers for a month; $100 will provide three families with nutritional supplements for a month; $200 will provide five children with baby formula for a month. You can also help the families by volunteering to run errands, shopping, babysitting during doctor visits, and helping out with children.

FACTS ABOUT WOMEN AND CHILDREN AND AIDS

- The number of women living with AIDS nearly doubled between 1994 and 1998.

- The proportion of new AIDS cases attributed to women tripled from 7 percent in 1985 to 23 percent in 1999.

- AIDS is the second leading cause of death among African American women ages twenty-five to forty-four; it is the third leading cause of death among Hispanic women in the same age group.

- More than 90 percent of children diagnosed with AIDS acquire the disease as a result of mother-to-infant transmission.

- It is estimated that two American teenagers are infected with HIV every hour of every day.

- Youth of color are overrepresented among youth with AIDS. African Americans and Latinos account for 69 percent of AIDS cases among youth ages thirteen to nineteen.

❧ WORDS OF WISDOM ❧

"Nothing nurtures language skills as well as reading aloud to a child."

—JIM TRELEASE, AUTHOR OF
THE READ-ALOUD HANDBOOK

23
Donate Food to Your Local Food Bank

Close your eyes and imagine a group of five children. Now consider these statistics:

- One out of every five children in America lives at or below the poverty line.
- One out of every five people in a soup kitchen line is a child.
- One out of every five children goes hungry part of every month.

These staggering statistics need to be changed. Children who are denied an adequate diet are at a greater risk than other low-income children of not reaching their full potential as individuals. Children who are undernourished have trouble concentrating and bonding with other children. They are more likely to suffer illnesses that force them to be absent from school. They consistently perform more poorly on standardized tests than their well-fed classmates. Studies have shown time and again that even mildly undernourished children may suffer abnormal cognitive and psychological development that, if not corrected, can be irreversible. Childhood hunger can have lifelong repercussions.

PARENTING TIP

A child learns from example.

Donate a bag of groceries to your local food bank. Call your local church, synagogue, or mosque to inquire about the closest food bank in your area.

To learn more about childhood hunger and what you can do to stop it, contact America's Second Harvest, 35 East Wacker Drive, #2000, Chicago, IL 60601; call (800)

771–2303; or visit the website *www.secondharvest.org*; or contact the Campaign to End Childhood Hunger at the Food Research and Action Center, 1875 Connecticut Avenue, N.W., Suite 540, Washington, DC 20009; call (202) 986–2200; or visit the website *www.frac.org*.

IF YOU CAN DO MORE: Organize a food drive with others in your community. Volunteer at a food pantry or kitchen. At most facilities you can choose to work back in the kitchen or with clients serving food and cleaning up. Thousands of children in America are going to bed hungry tonight; you can help.

FOOD FOR THOUGHT

- In 1999, approximately 12 million American children were food insecure, meaning they were hungry or at risk of hunger.

- Fully 46 percent of food-recipient households with children include at least one child under age five.

- 9 percent of food-recipient households report that children have missed meals in the past month because the family didn't have enough food or the means to obtain food.

- In 2000, requests for emergency food assistance from families with children increased by 16 percent in American cities over the past year, the highest increase since the recession of 1991.

- In 1999, more than half of all food stamp recipients —9.3 million people—were children.

- During the 1999–2000 school year, more than 15 million low-income children received free or reduced-price meals through the National School Lunch Program.

- Nearly 9 million children in the United States live in working poor families.

"None is so great that he needs no help, and none is so small that he cannot give it."

—KING SOLOMON

24 Locks of Love

Children need to fit in with their peers. Every year thousands of children lose their hair for medical reasons, making it difficult for them to look and act like "regular" kids. Locks of Love helps restore self-esteem and confidence to these kids, allowing them to face the world and their friends without embarrassment.

Locks of Love is a nonprofit organization that provides hairpieces to financially disadvantaged children under the age of eighteen with medical hair loss. These custom-fitted hairpieces made entirely of human hair are provided free of charge or on a sliding scale basis. Donors provide the hair, volunteers staff the office, and the manufacturer hand-assembles each piece.

Children comprise more than 80 percent of the donors, making this a charity of children helping children.

Donated hair must be at least ten inches (preferably twelve inches) in length. It must be bundled in a ponytail or braid. It must be free of hair damage by chemical processing. It must be clean and dry, and placed in a plastic bag. It takes about twelve ponytails to make a single hairpiece. Donations of ponytails less than ten inches are sold to offset the cost of manufacture. The retail value of the hairpieces is $3,000.

Children from infancy to age eight get synthetic hair because their hair grows so fast.

For more information or to make a donation of hair or money, contact Locks of Love, 1640 South Congress

Avenue, Suite 104, Palm Springs, FL 33461; call (561) 963–1677; or visit the website *www.locksoflove.org*.

IF YOU CAN DO MORE: You may have only one head of hair to give, but you can coordinate a hair drive in your community or church.

❧ WORDS OF WISDOM ❧

"Children are given to us—on loan—for a very short period of time. They come to us like packets of flower seeds, with no pictures on the cover and no guarantees. We do not know what they will look like, act like, or have the potential to become. Our job, like the gardener's, is to meet their needs as best we can: to give proper nourishment, love, attention, and caring, and to hope for the best."

—Katharine Kersey

Donate Clothing and Supplies to Your Local Foster Care Group Home

Clothes make the man—and the child. Children who don't have well-fitting clothes and shoes suffer more than exposure to the elements; they suffer harm to their self-image and confidence. The half million children who live in foster care and group homes have limited resources to buy clothing and shoes; most would love to have something new to wear.

Call your state department of social services to get a list of the nearest foster care group homes near you, and see what they need. Or log on to *www.acf.dhhs.gov/programs/cb/parent/index/htm* to search for your state foster home licensing specialist. When donating items, keep in mind that most facilities have limited storage space; try not to donate winter clothes in summer and vice versa. Also, be sure to clean clothes before you donate them, or buy new items. This is an easy way to give, but it will make a big difference to the children in need.

IF YOU CAN DO MORE: Coordinate a clothing drive among parents in your community.

ஃ *WORDS OF WISDOM* ஃ

"Ultimately a great nation is a compassionate nation."

—DR. MARTIN LUTHER KING, JR.

The YMCA (Young Men's Christian Association)

The YMCA isn't just for men—it isn't just for the young—it's for you! The nation's 2,400 YMCAs have more than 17 million members, half female and half under the age of seventeen. There are 500,000 kids in YMCA child care, and many of these children live in families whose annual income is less than $25,000 a year.

PARENTING TIP
Music is good
for the mind!

Each YMCA is different. A YMCA in your community may offer child care or teen leadership clubs, while a Y in the next town may have a swimming pool or art lessons. Every Y makes its own decisions about what programs to offer and how to operate to meet the needs of the community. Fees also vary, but financial assistance is available.

The YMCA is always looking for dedicated people to be volunteers, staff, members, and donors. It's the people of the YMCA who build strong kids, strong families, and strong communities.

More than 600,000 volunteers keep the YMCAs running nationwide. As a volunteer, you can lead an exercise class, read to preschoolers, coach a basketball team, design a program brochure, fill in at the front desk—the possibilities are endless. For information about your nearest YMCA, call (888) 333–YMCA, or visit the website *www.ymca.net.*

IF YOU CAN DO MORE: No Y nearby? Consider starting a new YMCA in your community. Every facility is volunteer founded and volunteer led. Information about starting a new facility is on the website.

Partners in Education: Adopt-a-School

Education is one of the most important aspects of a child's life. Partners in Education was developed nationally to address the needs of schoolchildren. It's an affiliation between schools and business, government, and civic leaders, designed to improve the quality of education for children everywhere. Partners in Education represents more than 7 million volunteers in more than 400,000 partnerships nationwide.

But you don't have to be a corporation to adopt a school. Individuals can do it. Every program sets its own objectives. Some partnerships provide mentors and tutors for students, establish citizenship and achievement awards, enlist volunteers to paint school libraries or help with library operations, donate office supplies and used or obsolete equipment, or perhaps simply coordinate volunteers to read to children. It can be that simple, but every effort helps make our schools a little bit better.

For more information on how to get involved, contact the National Association of Partners in Education, 901 Pitt Street, Suite 320, Alexandria, VA 22314; call (703) 836–4880; or visit the website *www.partnersineducation.org*. You can also call your local school district office and ask about the Adopt-a-School program in your area.

> **PARENTING TIP**
> Teach your children values: respect, compassion, and trust.

IF YOU CAN DO MORE: You can join Partners in Education as a volunteer member for $25 a year. This gives you a subscription to the national newsletter *Keeping Children at the Center* and it provides volunteer liability insurance. You can also work to coordinate a partnership between your place of work and a local school.

೫ *WORDS OF WISDOM* ೫

"Let us reform our schools, and we shall find little reform needed in our prisons."

—JOHN RUSKIN

28
Boys & Girls Clubs

In every community boys and girls are left to find their own recreation and companionship in the streets. An increasing number of children are at home with no adult care or supervision. These young people need to know that someone cares about them and someone has time for them.

The Boys & Girls Clubs are a safe place to learn and grow—and a lot of fun, too. The organization motto says it all: A Positive Place for Kids. The club programs and services promote and enhance a sense of competence, usefulness, and belonging.

The Boys & Girls Clubs of America was founded in 1860 by several women in Hartford, Connecticut, who believed that boys who roamed the streets should have a positive alternative. Over the years other clubs have been established with the goal of promoting the positive and healthy development of youth, especially those from disadvantaged circumstances.

> **PARENTING TIP**
> Tell your kids
> what they're
> doing right!

The clubs provide services that build the skills, civility, and self-confidence necessary to succeed in a competitive world. They provide a wide range of recreational, social, and pre-employment services to as many children and youths as possible during afternoons, evenings, and weekends in the neighborhoods in which they live. The clubs now serve 3.3 million children at more than 2,500 clubs nationwide.

Boys & Girls Clubs offers a variety of programs: Smart Moves, which provides drug and alcohol abuse prevention activities; Kids C.A.F.E., which feeds lunches to neighborhood children and teens; Fifth Dimension, a program that provides computer skills; and Power Hour, which provides homework help and educational reinforcement activities. Most importantly, the clubs offer a place where kids can be kids.

You can help the Boys & Girls Clubs with sponsorships, specific club programs, donated products, and cash contributions. For more information, contact Boys & Girls Clubs of America, 1230 West Peachtree Street, N.W., Atlanta, GA 30309; call (404) 487–5700 or (800) 854–CLUB; or visit the website *www.bgca.org*.

IF YOU CAN DO MORE: You can volunteer with a club in your area or, if one does not exist, you can find out about working to establish one.

ఴ *WORDS OF WISDOM* ఴ

"When you cease to make a contribution you begin to die."

—ELEANOR ROOSEVELT

29
Junior Achievement

Most kids crave opportunity. They want to be successful. They dream big about the future and believe they can be whatever they want to be when they grow up. Junior Achievement helps kids realize their dreams and their potential.

For more than eighty years, Junior Achievement has been helping young people sort out their choices in life and learn the skills necessary to reach their highest goals. The program teaches young people about business, economics, and free enterprise.

Since 1919, Junior Achievement has had an impact on more than 30 million young people. The organization is dedicated to providing programs that give business guidance to students. Through teams of classroom volunteers, Junior Achievement empowers youth by teaching them essential lessons that not only help them build careers, but also show them how to enjoy and appreciate free enterprise.

PARENTING TIP
Tell your children you are proud of them.

Junior Achievement programs span grades K–12, with age-appropriate curricula designed to teach elementary students about their roles as individuals, workers, and consumers, and to prepare middle and high school students for key economic and workforce issues they will face. Junior Achievement also teaches young people about the importance of staying in school.

Junior Achievement sponsors more than 150 affiliates nationwide, and Junior Achievement programs are used by teachers in more than 162,000 classrooms. The group's 100,000 classroom volunteers come from all walks of life and include businesspeople, college students, and retirees. No matter what your age or work status, you have something to offer.

Junior Achievement is building a better world—one student at a time—and you can help. To find a Junior Achievement near you, contact Junior Achievement, Inc., One Education Way, Colorado Springs, CO 80906; call (719) 540–8000 or (800) 843–6395; or visit the website *www.ja.org.*

IF YOU CAN DO MORE: Preparing children for the economic realities of the twenty-first century is the responsibility of everyone in the community. The Junior Achievement office near you can provide materials and training so that you can get into the classroom and begin teaching. To broaden the impact of your involvement, you could work with a team of volunteers to create or expand a dynamic program in a school or at several grade levels.

ᘐ *WORDS OF WISDOM* ᘐ

"Although the world is full of suffering, it is full also of the overcoming of it."

—HELEN KELLER

Girl Scouts and Boy Scouts of America

Scouting can help both girls and boys develop into mature, well-balanced, and responsible citizens. And the kids have lots of fun together, too.

Girl Scouts is one of the world's leading organizations dedicated solely to girls. For ninety years, committed professionals and volunteers have worked together to help girls grow strong in body, mind, and spirit. Girls develop strong values, a social conscience, and the conviction of their own potential and self-worth. Activities promote the development of leadership and decision-making skills. Programs such as the annual cookie sale help girls learn how to set goals and reach them. The programs serve girls ages five to seventeen.

PARENTING TIP
Notice your children!

To find out how to help, contact the organization at (800) GSUSA4U or visit the website *www.girlscouts.org*.

Boy Scouts of America provides quality youth programs, time-tested to insure that the boys and young men who participate in them have the best opportunity to become fine citizens, strong family members, and community leaders. The National Council of the Boy Scouts of America supports more than three hundred local councils that provide a range of scouting programs, including Tiger Cubs, Cub Scouts, Boy Scouts, and Venturing.

Learn about volunteer possibilities. Contact Boy Scouts of America, National Council, P.O. Box 152079, Irving, TX 75015–2079; call (213) 413–4400; or visit the website *www.bsa.scouting.org.*

IF YOU CAN DO MORE: You can help out with special events, or make an ongoing commitment to a group of children by starting a scout troop or pack in your community. Both Girl Scouts and Boys Scouts offer training to interested volunteers.

❧ *WORDS OF WISDOM* ❧

"Our duty is to be useful, not according to our desires but according to our power."

–Amiel, Journal, December 17, 1856

31
Toys For Tots

The Toys For Tots program is one of the nation's most compelling charitable success stories. Established as the Marine Corps's community action program, they've been the unchallenged leaders in looking after needy children at Christmastime for fifty-one years.

Local campaigns begin in October and run until December 22. Members of the community drop off new, unwrapped toys in collection boxes located at local businesses. Toys For Tots coordinators, with assistance from local welfare agencies and community groups, distribute the toys to the neediest children in the community.

PARENTING TIP
Ask for
your children's
opinions.

Toys For Tots plays an important role in helping children emerge from a background of poverty to adulthood with a positive attitude and hope for their future. Toys For Tots has a positive impact on communities. It's one way busy Americans can help to bring about a change for our nation's needy youth, and you can help. During the first campaign in 1947, 5,000 toys were collected in Los Angeles for needy kids. In 2000, more than 15.8 million toys were collected and distributed to more than 6.3 million needy children.

For more information, contact Marine Toys For Tots Foundation, P.O. Box 1947, Quantico, VA 22134; call (703) 640–9433; or visit the website *www.toysfortots.org*.

IF YOU CAN DO MORE: Local campaigns are conducted in more than three hundred communities in all fifty states. In each location a Marine reservist or a member of a local organization is designated Toys For Tots Coordinator, and that person is responsible for organizing and conducting the campaign in the community. You can contact that person and volunteer to help with the campaign, perhaps by recruiting stores to sponsor collection boxes or by sorting toys and preparing them for distribution.

❧ *WORDS OF WISDOM* ❧

"Do what you can, with what you have, where you are."

—THEODORE ROOSEVELT

UNICEF (United Nations Children's Fund)

For more than fifty years, this global organization has helped governments, communities, and families in 161 countries make better, safe, healthier places for children.

UNICEF was established by the United Nations to meet the emergency needs of children in postwar Europe and China. In 1950 its mandate broadened to address long-term needs of children and mothers in developing countries. In 1953, the United Nations International Children's Emergency Fund was given a permanent status and its name was changed to the United Nations Children's Fund, though the acronym UNICEF was kept.

PARENTING TIP

Keep the promises you make.

As part of its ongoing efforts, UNICEF is a major force in advocating for children's rights, helping to provide immunizations, making pregnancy and childbirth safe, and encouraging the care and stimulation needed to give a child the best possible start in life. UNICEF works hard to bring ideas, resources, and support to the areas where they are needed most. The group is nonpartisan and does not discriminate.

You can support UNICEF with donations as well as support its fundraising through the sale of UNICEF cards, calendars, and stationery. For more information, contact The United States Fund for UNICEF, 333 East 38th Street, GC–6, New York, NY 10016; call (212) 686–5522; or visit the website *www.unicef.org*.

IF YOU CAN DO MORE: You can volunteer for UNICEF. For more information, see the UNICEF employment pages on the website.

❧ *WORDS OF WISDOM* ❧

"Treat people as if they were what they ought to be and you help them to become what they're capable of being."

—GOETHE

Offer a Job to an Emancipated Youth

It is almost impossible to overstate the importance of the eighteenth birthday: Go to bed a seventeen-year-old child; wake up in the morning an official adult. While most children enter adulthood with the support of a family offering emotional and financial help when needed, children in foster care come of age without a safety net. In the eyes of the law, when children "age out" of foster care, they are "emancipated" and must find a job and pay for their own education, clothing, housing, and food.

During the transition into adulthood, many of the 13,000 to 20,000 youth who are dropped from the child welfare system each year still need a helping hand. Without intervention, 40 to 50 percent of emancipated youth become homeless, many within a year. Studies have found that emancipated youth suffer disproportionately from ill health, poor education, homelessness, substance abuse, and criminal behavior. Many former foster youth do not graduate from high school, leaving them without sufficient skills to secure a decent paying job. Half have trouble finding enough money to pay for food and housing. One-third have done something illegal to get money, including stealing, prostitution, or selling drugs.

PARENTING TIP

Make time to be with your children; they will grow up before you know it.

Bridges to Independence in Los Angeles has served emancipated youth for years. The program is a collaboration between the Los Angeles County Department of Children and Family Services, the United Friends of the

Children Bridges, and the Weingart Foundation. The trail-blazing program assists these special young adults with housing, career placement, and education.

One way you can help emancipated youth in your area is to offer them entry-level jobs at your place of business. Providing a young person with the opportunity to earn a living could be all that it takes to turn his or her life in the right direction. These kids need a chance to make it, and you can help. Contact the human resources department at your place of employment and ask that someone there alert the nearest social services agency that you have job openings in areas where a youth could be trained. It could be that simple.

For more information on how you can assist a child in life after foster care, contact your local foster care agency. (For more information on foster care, see chapter 49.) If you would like more information about United Friends of the Children Bridges, call (310) 338–3646 or send an e-mail to *ufcbridges@aol.com*.

> **IF YOU CAN DO MORE:** Children who have been pushed out of the foster care system may not be ready for the challenges of adulthood. Consider taking one or more emancipated youth under your wing and help them find employment, training, scholarship aid, and other transitional assistance. Be a mentor; help guide them toward responsible behavior and encourage them along the way. Be a mentor, a role model, a friend. You may be the only person watching out for that child, and your efforts could make all the difference in what kind of adult that child becomes.

ॐ *WORDS OF WISDOM* ॐ

"Every calling is great when greatly pursued."

—OLIVER WENDELL HOLMES, JR.

34 Starlight Children's Foundation

When a child has a serious illness and is confined to a hospital bed, the days can drag—and the lonely nights can be worse. Studies have found that distractive entertainment programs actually reduce pain and lessen the requests for pain medication. The Starlight Foundation tries to ease the pain experienced by seriously, chronically, and terminally ill children by providing state-of-the-art audiovisual entertainment and granting special wishes.

Organized in 1983, the Starlight Children's Foundation's mission is to bring joy to children who are dealing with the trauma of a serious illness. Working with more than 650 hospitals worldwide, the foundation provides an impressive menu of both in-hospital and outpatient programs and services. The outpatient programs include Kids Activity Network outings and wish granting, and the in-patient programs include Fun Centers, Starlight Rooms, clown programs, and hospital parties, to name a few.

PARENTING TIP
Try not to
let anger guide
your actions.

It's a successful program. More than 74,000 children between the ages of four and eighteen worldwide benefit from the foundation's programs and services every month. The international headquarters are in Los Angeles, but the Starlight Children's Foundation has a network of chapters located in the United States, the United Kingdom, Australia, and Canada.

You can help to make a very ill child feel a little better. For more information, contact the International Headquarters Starlight Children's Foundation, 5900

Wilshire Boulevard, Suite 2530, Los Angeles, CA 90036; call (323) 634–0080; or visit the website *www.starlight.org.*

IF YOU CAN DO MORE: You can use your skills and experience to help by contacting the foundation and finding out about programs in your area. You can donate your American Airlines Aadvantage Program Miles to help defray travel costs. Some Starlight volunteers coordinate special events; others help with wish granting or fundraising. Starlight provides training to help you learn more about the foundation and how you can help.

❧ WORDS OF WISDOM ❧
"We make a living by what we do, but we make a life by what we give."

—WINSTON CHURCHILL

35 Covenant House

Covenant House services are offered to all youth seeking help. No one is ever turned away, and each youth is accepted on a "no questions asked" basis. The shelters provide a place to sleep, food and clothing, and programs for helping to develop skills to prepare for independent adult living.

The first contact many youths have with Covenant House may be with members of the Van Outreach team, who travel the streets at night searching for homeless, frightened, disenfranchised youth. Others call the Nineline, a help line available for kids who need to talk: (800) 999–9999. Each year the Nineline receives more than 84,000 crisis calls from youth across the country who need help and have nowhere else to turn.

～

PARENTING TIP
Take time to play with your children.

～

Covenant House began in 1969 when a Franciscan priest, Father Bruce Ritter, provided a night of shelter in a snowstorm for six young runaways in his small apartment on the lower east side of Manhattan. Covenant House was founded in New York City in 1972 and has since expanded to Anchorage, Atlantic City, Detroit, Fort Lauderdale, Houston, Los Angeles, Newark, New Orleans, Oakland, Orlando, Philadelphia, St. Louis, Washington, D.C., and six cities outside the United States. Each year more than 50,000 kids come to Covenant House, making it the largest shelter program for homeless kids in the Americas.

Volunteer possibilities abound, and each Covenant House has a "wish list" for donations. Your contributions make a difference: $35 feeds one child for a week; $50 buys five blankets, $199 provides twenty-five nutritious turkey dinners. For more information, contact Covenant House, 1015 15th Street, N.W., Washington, DC 20005; call (202) 610–9600; or visit the website *www.covenanthouse.org.*

IF YOU CAN DO MORE: Volunteer to work with the outreach staff. Covenant House volunteers don't wait for kids to come to them. In vans, on bikes, and on foot, volunteers walk the same streets the kids do, offering food and help to kids in trouble. Some children pass up help one night, but come in the next.

❧ WORDS OF WISDOM ❧

"Let early education be a sort of amusement; you will then be better able to discover the child's natural bent."

—PLATO, THE REPUBLIC, CIRCA 375 B.C.

Partnership for a Drug-Free America

One of the toughest problems the youth of today face is the proliferation of drugs. With approximately 6 million Americans addicted to illegal drugs, it's clear we have to do something.

Partnership for a Drug-Free America has taken a stand. A private, nonprofit, nonpartisan coalition of professionals from the communications industry, the partnership is dedicated to reducing the demand for illicit drugs in America. Through its national antidrug advertising campaign and other forms of communication, the partnership works to decrease demand for drugs by changing societal attitudes that support or condone drug use.

PARENTING TIP
Get to know your child's friends.

Advertising agencies create partnership materials, and talent unions permit their members to work without a fee.

More than six hundred antidrug ads, worth more than $3 billion, have been created. In addition to the national work, the partnership has helped create more than fifty state- and city-based versions of the national campaign. Its programs and activities are funded by generous contributions from hundreds of individuals, foundations, and corporations.

You can help them spread the word against drugs. For more information, contact the Partnership for a Drug-Free America, 405 Lexington Avenue, 16th Floor, New York, NY 10174; call (212) 922–1560; or visit the website *www.drugfreeamerica.org.* (The website also includes good information about drugs and how to talk with your child about drugs.)

IF YOU CAN DO MORE: Talk to your kids about drugs. According to research, parents who are closely involved in their children's lives—knowing exactly where teens are, what they're doing, who their friends are—have children who are less likely to experiment with drugs.

JUST THE FACTS

According to the 2000 Partnership Attitude Tracking Study, there are about 23.6 million teens in grades 7 through 12 in America today.

- 11.3 million of them (48 percent of the teen population) have tried illegal drugs.

- 5.9 million of them (25 percent) have used illegal drugs in the past thirty days.

- 9.4 million teens (40 percent) have tried marijuana.

- 7.9 million teens (33 percent) have used marijuana in the past year.

✆ WORDS OF WISDOM ✆

"Man can see his reflection on water only when he bends down close to it; and the heart of man, too, must lean down to the heart of his fellow; then it will see itself within his heart."

—HASIDIC PROVERB

37
Shriners Hospitals for Children

A network of twenty-two hospitals, Shriners Hospitals for Children provide no-cost orthopedic, burn, and spinal cord injury care to children under age eighteen. There is never a charge to the patient, parent, or any third party for any service or medical treatment received at Shriners Hospitals, and children are treated without regard to race, religion, or relationship to a Shriner.

If you know of a child Shriners Hospitals might be able to help, call their patient referral line: (800) 237–5055 (in the United States) or (800) 361–7256 (in Canada). Children are accepted for treatment if, in the opinion of the chief of staff of the hospital, there is a reasonable possibility that treatment will benefit the child.

PARENTING TIP
Eat dinner with your child.

Shriners Hospitals have provided free medical care to more than 625,000 children since its founding in 1919.

When the Shriners first decided to establish the Shriners Hospital for Crippled Children, it was supported by a yearly $2 assessment from each Shriner. Today, the hospitals rely on support from other sources as well; your donations are welcomed.

For more information, contact International Shriners Headquarters, 2900 Rocky Point Drive, Tampa, FL 33607–1460; call (813) 281–0300; or visit the website *www.shriners.com*.

IF YOU CAN DO MORE: If you would like to work with children hospitalized with orthopedic problems, burns, or spinal cord injuries, contact the

Shriners Hospital nearest you. Volunteers are always needed to read to children, collect books or toys, or help out in other ways.

Part 3

Big Ways

Every act of charity transforms the world, at least a little bit. The ideas covered in this section tend to require a significant commitment of your time or resources, but they can make a dramatic difference in a child's life. Somewhere there is a child waiting for your help.

Big Brothers Big Sisters of America

The number of children growing up in one-parent homes is increasing each year, and the patterns of instability and upheaval in family life are expected to continue. But you can make a difference.

Big Brothers Big Sisters can provide the support and friendship so many children desperately need. The children matched with a Big Brother or Big Sister often come from extremely difficult situations. Fully 83 percent live at or below poverty level. Some 52 percent have alcoholic or drug-addicted family members. And 54 percent have been abused or neglected. Having a relationship with a caring adult can help these needy children reach their potential and fulfill their dreams.

PARENTING TIP
Read to your child every day.

The need is great. This is a wonderful way to make a big difference in the life of a child. Children who participate in the program do better in school, according to recent research. Teachers and parents report that kids show marked improvement in grades, attitudes, and relationships. Specifically, 64 percent of students who participated in the Big Brothers Big Sisters program developed more positive attitudes toward school; 58 percent achieved higher grades in social studies, languages, and math; 60 percent improved their relationships with adults; 56 percent improved relationships with peers; and 64 percent developed higher levels of self-confidence. Quite an impressive record.

For more information about how to become a Big

Brother or Big Sister, contact the National Office, 230 North 13th Street, Philadelphia, PA 19107; call (215) 567–7000; or visit the website *www.bigbrothersbigsisters.org.*

IF YOU CAN DO MORE: You could coordinate a group of friends or coworkers to volunteer with Big Brothers Big Sisters together. While you want each adult to develop a meaningful relationship with the child, having a group of friends to do some joint activities could be a lot of fun—and it might help more adults get involved.

❧ *WORDS OF WISDOM* ❧
"It is one of the most beautiful compensations of this life that no man can sincerely try to help another without helping himself."

—RALPH WALDO EMERSON

Community of Caring

Community of Caring is an organization founded by Eunice Kennedy Shriver and developed by a group of philosophers, educators, health specialists, legal professionals, ethicists, policy makers, and psychologists. The goal is to get the community to work together with the schools to make a difference in the lives of children living in difficult situations. Community of Caring addresses destructive attitudes that can lead to early sexual involvement, teen pregnancy, substance abuse, delinquent behavior, and school failure.

↩
PARENTING TIP
Delight in the discoveries of your children.
↩

Community of Caring builds its program around five basic values: care, respect, responsibility, trust, and family. Community of Caring strives to promote these values and incorporate them into our families, schools, and communities.

Community of Caring schools weave discussions about values into the existing curriculum. The goal is to help young people understand the relationships among their values, decisions, and actions. The five values are demonstrated and discussed in relation to real-life, tough situations that students encounter every day; they focus on ways they can use the five values to affect their life choices and behavior.

Students in three Community of Caring schools raised their grade point averages by 43 percent, 46 percent, and 71 percent. Students in a Community of Caring program show greater gains in knowledge about the adverse consequences and risks of early sexual activity.

For more information about ways to support the program, contact Community of Caring, 1325 G Street, N.W., Suite 500, Washington, DC 20005; call (202) 393–1251; or visit the website *www.communityofcaring.org*.

IF YOU CAN DO MORE: Every year at least a hundred schools decide to become Community of Caring schools. The process can be started by a teacher, administrator, or parent; but it requires commitment from teachers, administrators, students, and parents. If you are willing to work on bringing the program to your school, you will have to work with both the national office of Community of Caring and local school officials, who will have to underwrite training costs for the program.

❧ WORDS OF WISDOM ❧

"If we do not bequeath to them something worth calling life, then we cannot expect of them any lives that are worthwhile."

—THE REV. DR. GARDNER TAYLOR

THE FIVE COMMUNITY OF CARING VALUES

1. **Caring:** Caring is the opposite of both indifference and hate. Caring is at the heart of a decent life.

2. **Responsibility:** People who are caring must be willing to take responsibility. That means they are accountable for their actions, enjoying praise when things go well and accepting blame when things go wrong. This is a sign of maturity.

3. **Respect:** If I take responsibility for myself, others will begin to respect me. I can also respect others who stand up for what they believe is right. Respect for each other makes a moral community and a community of caring possible.

4. **Trust:** When people care for and respect each other, trust grows. Trusting people also means counting on them: depending on them and expecting them to deliver. Communities of people cannot exist without a certain level of trust.

5. **Family:** We begin to learn our values in our families. Family is the "school of character," where values are taught and learned.

Create a Scholarship Fund

Not every young person has the financial resources to go to college. You—or you as a member of a business, professional group, or civic association—can help by creating a scholarship fund for a worthy young person. Even a scholarship of $500 can go a long way toward helping a family meet the high costs of a college education.

You can raise funds by organizing a scholarship fundraising drive. Ask willing coworkers or friends to donate whatever they can. Organize the fundraiser as a holiday gift that you give to your community. No matter how much you raise, it will be well received. Let your employees know that their efforts have made it possible for at least one student to pay for part of their longed-for college education.

↶

PARENTING TIP
Love your
children, no
matter what.

↷

Before starting your fundraising effort, you will want to establish the criteria for selecting a qualified recipient. Do you want to reward academic performance? Community service? You want to consider ways of recruiting applicants. Do you want young people to apply directly? Do you want teachers or principals to nominate students? Do you want applications open to community members to name worthy children? It's up to you to decide how you want the program to operate.

You may create a one-time scholarship, a fund that requires an annual fundraising event, or even an endowed scholarship fund to honor or memorialize an individual on an ongoing basis. (With an endowed scholarship, a fixed percentage of the endowment earnings are used to fund the scholarship.) All donations are tax deductible.

If you wish, you could also include a scholarship endowment as part of your will. You could write a bequest for a specific amount of money to go into a scholarship fund.

IF YOU CAN DO MORE: If you wish to make a large scholarship fund, you might consider using more elaborate financial mechanisms. You could fund a scholarship using life insurance, an annuity, a charitable remainder trust, or other planned giving instruments.

SCHOLARSHIP FACTS

· More than $37 billion in college financial aid is available through the federal government.

· There are more than 600,000 college scholarships available.

· More than $6.6 billion in scholarship money goes unclaimed each year because eligible students do not apply. Be sure to advertise your scholarship widely.

ℱ℘ *WORDS OF WISDOM* ℘ℱ
"We can do no great things—only small things with great love."

—Mother Teresa

CASA (National Court Appointed Special Advocate for Children)

All too often, a judge must make a decision about an abused or neglected child's future without knowing all the facts about the case. Frustrated with this situation, a Seattle judge conceived the idea of using trained community volunteers to speak for the best interests of these children in court.

The program was so successful that judges across the country began borrowing the idea. In 1990 the U.S. Congress encouraged the program with the passage of the Victims of Child Abuse Act. Today, more than 42,000 volunteers represent the needs of children through a network of CASA— Court Appointed Special Advocate— programs, which operate nationwide.

CASA volunteers are ordinary people who care about kids. They come from all backgrounds and ages, and they need no legal expertise to serve. After a forty-hour training course, a CASA volunteer is assigned to an abuse or neglect case by a judge. The volunteer conducts thorough research on the background of the case, reviews documents, and interviews everyone involved, including the child. Your job is not to act as a big brother, big sister, or friend; it is to determine what action should be taken to protect the child. CASA advocates then make reports to the court, recommending what they believe is best for the child, providing the judge with information

PARENTING TIP

Remind your child of the many ways she is special.

that will help to make an informed decision. CASA volunteers can also be instrumental in assuring that a child or family receives court-ordered services, such as educational testing or substance abuse counseling.

During a case, a CASA volunteer monitors the child's situation and makes sure the child is safe. CASA volunteers may be the only constant the child knows as she moves through the labyrinth of the child welfare system.

When you take on a case, you take on a child's future. Most programs ask for a commitment of at least a year. Some cases take longer. The amount of time a case requires varies, depending on the stage of the proceedings. Nationally, CASA volunteers give an average of eighty-eight hours a year—about ten hours doing research and conducting interviews prior to the first court appearance. More complicated cases may take longer. Once initiated into the system, volunteers work about ten to fifteen hours a month.

You can support CASA's vital work by becoming a member of the national organization; the dues are $25 a year. For more information about joining or volunteering, contact The National CASA Association, 100 West Harrison Street, North Tower, Suite 500, Seattle, WA 98119; call (800) 628–3233; or visit the website *www.national-casa.org.*

IF YOU CAN DO MORE: CASA relies on volunteer supervisors and program directors to coordinate programs in every state. These supervisors are available to discuss your case, help solve problems, and make sure you get any legal support you need. Many programs have mentor components in which experienced volunteers are matched up with new volunteers.

"*A teacher affects eternity; he can never tell where his influence stops.*"

—HENRY ADAMS

42 Habitat for Humanity

Every child deserves a home. Nearly 30 million U.S. households face housing problems, including cost burdens, overcrowding, or run-down conditions, such as no hot water, no electricity, or no toilet. Some 3.9 million children live in "worst-case" housing, according to the U.S. Department of Housing and Urban Development.

Habitat for Humanity International strives to provide shelter for families around the world. Habitat has built more than 100,000 houses, providing more than 500,000 people in more than 2,000 communities with safe, decent, affordable shelter.

✐
PARENTING TIP
Expect the best
from your children,
but don't expect
perfection.
✐

Through volunteer labor and donations of money and materials, Habitat builds and rehabilitates basic houses with the help of the homeowner partner families. Habitat houses are sold to partner families at no profit, financed with affordable, no-interest loans. The homeowner's monthly mortgage payments are used to build more Habitat houses.

Habitat is not a giveaway program. In addition to a down payment and monthly mortgage payments, homeowners invest hundreds of hours of their own labor—sweat equity—into building their Habitat house and the houses of others.

Throughout the world, the cost of houses varies from as little as $800 in some developing countries to an average of $46,600 in the United States. Habitat houses are affordable for low-income families because there is no profit included in the sale price and no interest charged on the mortgages.

Habitat accomplishes this goal at the community level by working with affiliates—independent, locally run, non-profit organizations. Each affiliate coordinates all aspects of Habitat home building in its local area—fundraising, building site selections, partner family selection and support, house constructions, and mortgage servicing. There are more than 1,900 active affiliates in 79 countries, including all 50 states, the District of Columbia, Guam, and Puerto Rico. The Habitat for Humanity International headquarters provides training and support to affiliates worldwide.

To help, you can pick up a hammer and help with home construction, make a donation, or help with administrative tasks. To locate a local affiliate or learn more about Habitat, contact Habitat for Humanity International, 121 Habitat Street, Americus, GA 31709–3498; call (800) 422–4826; (229) 924–6935; or visit the website *www.habitat.org.*

IF YOU CAN DO MORE: Habitat affiliates start when concerned citizens of diverse backgrounds come together to address the problem of poverty housing in their community. These volunteers research the community's affordable housing needs and resources, and evaluate the potential success of a Habitat self-help model in their community. The group then applies to Habitat to become an affiliate. If your area does not have an affiliate and needs one, contact the office about establishing a Habitat affiliate in your area.

❧ *WORDS OF WISDOM* ❧

"The highest service we can perform for others is to help them help themselves."

—Horace Mann

THE FACTS ABOUT AFFORDABLE HOUSING IN THE U.S.

- About 2.5 million Americans live in overcrowded homes, meaning the number of people living in the house is greater than the total number of rooms.

- One family in seven lives in housing that is severely inadequate, meaning it has deficiencies such as no hot water, no electricity, no toilet, and/or no bathtub or shower.

- More than 6.7 million households pay more than 50 percent of their income for rent.

- Between 1997 and 1999, there was a 9 percent drop in the number of rental units available to very low income renters.

- To afford the medial fair-market price of a two-bedroom rental unit in the United States, a worker would have to earn a wage of $12.47 per hour, or nearly two and a half times more than the current federal minimum wage.

- For 14.8 million U.S. households that make $10,000 or less per year, a year's rent is about 70 percent of their annual income.

OVERSEAS

- The United Nations Center for Human Settlements estimates that 1.1 billion people live in inadequate housing in urban areas alone.

- In Latin America, households need 5.4 times their annual income to buy a house. In Africa, they need an average of 12.5 times their annual income.

- Less than 20 percent of households in Africa are connected to piped water.

- Less than 35 percent of cities in the developing world have their wastewater treated.

43 RIF (Reading Is Fundamental)

Reading Is Fundamental helps motivate school-age children to learn to read. The grassroots network of more than 360,000 volunteers provides new, free books and other literacy resources to more than 5 million children and their families. The program focuses on needy children from infancy to age eleven; many RIF kids have learning needs or economic limitations that put them at risk of failing to succeed in school. (More than 60 percent of high school dropouts are not literate.)

〜
PARENTING TIP
Enjoy the great
outdoors with
your child.
〜

The program relies on dedicated volunteers, typically parents, teachers, librarians, and other interested citizens. Since RIF was founded in 1966, the program has placed more than 200 million books in the hands of interested children.

RIF works with the U.S. Department of Education and local organizations to purchase books at a discount. Children in the program are able to choose and keep several free paperback books each year.

RIF also sponsors several other programs, including Shared Beginnings, which encourages teen parents to read to their infants; Family of Readers, which works with families of children from birth to age eight to encourage a love of reading; Care to Read, which provides training staff of home-based child care programs; and RIF Book Clubs, an informal read-aloud program for young children.

RIF volunteers select and order books, organize book events, read books aloud and tell stories, plan reading activities, raise awareness of literacy in the community, and raise funds.

For more information, contact Reading Is Fund-amental, Inc., 1825 Connecticut Avenue, N.W., Suite 400, Washington, DC 20009; call (877) RIF–READ or (202) 287–3220; or visit the website *www.rif.org*.

IF YOU CAN DO MORE: If none of RIF's 16,500 programs is in your area, consider starting one. You may schedule your program to run year-round, during the school year, or for the summer. You can run the program from a school, library, child care center, park, or any other place children gather.

WORDS OF WISDOM
"The be-all and end-all of life should not be to get rich, but to enrich the world."

—B. C. FORBES

Heifer Project International

In the 1930s, a civil war raged in Spain. Dan West, a mid-western farmer and Church of the Brethren youth worker, ladled out cups of milk to hungry children on both sides of the conflict. It struck him that what these families needed was "not a cup, but a cow." He asked his friends back home to donate heifers, young cows that have not borne a calf, so hungry families could feed themselves. In return, they could help another family become self-reliant by passing on to them one of their gift animal's female calves.

PARENTING TIP
Enjoy the moment.

The idea of giving families a source of food rather than short-term relief caught on and has continued for more than fifty years. As a result, families in 115 countries have enjoyed better health, more income, and the joy of helping others. Children receive milk and eggs; families earn income for school, health care, and better housing; communities fulfill their dreams; and farmers learn sustainable, environmentally sound agricultural techniques.

Heifer Project International provides appropriate livestock, training, and related service to small-scale farmers worldwide. The program helps people use livestock as an integral part of sustainable agriculture and holistic development.

Heifer Project's key concept is that each recipient must pass on to others some of the offspring of the farm animals they receive. This principle, called "passing on the gift," ensures that each participant in the program becomes a donor, enhancing dignity and participation in the project.

Passing on the gift also helps communities become self-sustaining.

When you make a donation, you are given an honor card or gift card to tell your friends and family about the special gifts you have given in their name. For more information, contact Heifer Project International, P.O. Box 8058, Little Rock, AR 72203; call (800) 422–0474; or visit the website *www.heiferproject.org.*

> **IF YOU CAN DO MORE:** Rather than give a single animal, why not sponsor an entire "ark"? Work with a civic or religious group to raise funds for an ark filled with animals. You can also arrange to contribute monthly through an automatic withdrawal from either a checking account or credit card. You can also volunteer overseas; however, you must cover all of your expenses, including travel, lodging, insurance, and daily living expenses.

FILL AN ARK
Heifer Project Arks include the following animals:

2 flocks of chicks	2 goats
2 sheep	2 oxen
2 trios of rabbits	2 cows
2 beehives	2 trios of ducks
2 guinea pigs	2 water buffalo
2 llamas	2 flocks of geese
2 camels	2 pigs
2 donkeys	

❧ WORDS OF WISDOM ❧
"I feel the greatest reward for doing is the opportunity to do more."
—JONAS SALK

Participate Weekly at Your Child's School

You don't need to travel long distances or write out large checks to support your child's school. In fact, at most schools getting involved is as simple as calling the office or dropping by for a visit and asking what you can do to help.

You may find it useful to get involved with your school's Parent Teacher Association or Parent Teacher Organization. These groups may already have volunteer possibilities lined up for you. Both public and private schools need volunteers, so don't be shy about offering a helping hand to a private school.

In addition, most teachers would appreciate an extra set of hands to help their classrooms run smoothly. Many teachers face large class sizes and little support, so your contributions would be well received. Parents can help with these needs. Sign up to help at school once a week. It'll make a huge difference for your child and your child's teacher.

> **PARENTING TIP**
> Encourage your child to help others.

> **IF YOU CAN DO MORE:** In this case, if some is good, more really is better. Teachers appreciate volunteer help once a week—but twice a week is even better. Give as much time as possible; studies show that low teacher-student ratios increase academic performance. Your presence in the classroom will enrich the achievement of all the children in your child's class.

COMMON VOLUNTEER OPPORTUNITIES AT SCHOOL

Talk to your child's teacher about specific ways to help. The following are some volunteer positions offered at many schools:

· Library aid: Place returned books on shelves, straighten shelves, do clerical work, help children choose books.

· Art assistance: Prepare materials, distribute supplies, help with clean-up.

· Absentee call-in: Record student absences, check with parents who did not let the school know their child would be absent.

· Cafeteria and recess aid: Monitor children during lunch and on the playground.

· Classroom aid: Support the teacher as needed; for example, help with special projects, assist with classroom parties, offer one-on-one tutoring with children who need special help.

· Computer enrichment: Assist children as they learn how to work on the computers.

· Office assistance: Make copies, answer phones, assist with clerical work.

For more information about getting involved with your child's school, contact the National PTA at 330 North Wabash Avenue, Suite 2100, Chicago, IL 60611; call (800) 307–4PTA; or visit the website *www.pta.org*.

ℱ๑ *WORDS OF WISDOM* ℱ๑

"There are only two lasting bequests we can hope to give our children. One of these is roots, the other, wings."

—HODDING CARTER

Be a Mentor

Children naturally turn to the adults around them for support, encouragement, and guidance. People who act in this role for others are often called mentors.

A mentor is a person who, along with a child's parents, provides a young person with support, counsel, friendship, reinforcement, and constructive example. Mentors are good listeners, people who care, people who want to help young people build on their strengths to succeed in life. A mentor is a guide, a friend, a listener, a coach. Mentors help youngsters stay in school, achieve their goals, and avoid unsafe activities.

Mentoring benefits all of society. A child who has a mentor has a better chance of growing up to be a healthy, educated, and productive adult, and, eventually, a responsible parent. According to research, young people who meet regularly with a mentor are 46 percent less likely to begin using drugs; 27 percent less likely to begin drinking alcohol; 52 percent less likely to skip school; and 33 percent less likely to hit someone. Mentoring makes a big difference.

Mentors are ordinary people. A mentor is someone who cares, who listens, who offers encouragement. Mentors help kids develop their strengths and talents. Mentors provide additional support for a child struggling to navigate through the rocky seas of childhood. You don't need special skills to be an effective mentor. Things that seem easy or straightforward to you are often mysterious to young people. That's why it can be easier than you think to make a difference in a young person's life.

Think about how you want to work with a young person. What activities interest you? What age do you want to work with? Do you want to work one-on-one or try coaching or leadership with a group? How much time do you want to give? Most mentoring programs look for a commitment of at least six months.

There are more than five thousand mentoring programs nationwide. To search a database of local mentoring programs in your area or to learn more about becoming a mentor, contact the National Mentoring Partnership, 1600 Duke Street, Suite 300, Alexandria, VA 22314; call (703) 224–2200 or toll-free (877) BE–A–MENTOR; or visit the website *www.mentoring.org*.

> **IF YOU CAN DO MORE:** While mentoring involves finding the right match between adults and children, you can help to develop a match-making service on a local level by compiling mentoring opportunities in your area and sharing them with friends or coworkers. Mentoring with a friend can make the process more fun for everyone.

☙ WORDS OF WISDOM ☙

"Giving frees us from the familiar territory of our own needs by opening our minds to the unexplored worlds occupied by the needs of others."

—BARBARA HAND HERRERA

AmeriCorps

Put your idealism to work: tutor a child; build a playground; work with police to make neighborhoods safer; help build or rehabilitate homes; plant trees; remove trash from neighborhoods; take children to be immunized; work in clinics, VA hospitals, or other health-care facilities—the possibilities to do good works are virtually endless. Whatever your interests, AmeriCorps can help you find a program that needs your energy and dedication.

AmeriCorps—sometimes referred to as the domestic Peace Corps—is a national network of hundreds of programs through the U.S. Volunteers work through AmeriCorps, but they work for groups such as the American Red Cross, Habitat for Humanity, Boys & Girls Clubs of America, and other established local and national service projects. AmeriCorps manages two major programs:

- **AmeriCorps VISTA** (Volunteers in Service to America) members work in low-income communities. Volunteers serve full-time and live in the communities they serve; they create programs that continue after they complete their service.
- **AmeriCorps NCCC** (National Civilian Community Corps) members work in projects involving education, public safety, the environment, and other human needs. This ten-month, full-time residential program is for people ages eighteen to twenty-four; the program combines civilian service with certain

aspects of military service, such as leadership and team building.

(Peace Corps volunteers work overseas for two years at a time. For more information on the Peace Corps, visit their website at *www.peacecorps.gov.*)

You must be seventeen or older to sign up with AmeriCorps. For your time and trouble, you are paid a modest living allowance; some programs provide housing. In addition, for a term of service with AmeriCorps, members can earn an education award of up to $4,725 that can be used for student loan repayment and school tuition.

More than 100,000 Americans have served or are now serving as AmeriCorps members. For more information about AmeriCorps, contact Corporation for National Service, 1201 New York Avenue, N.W., Washington, DC 20525; call (202) 606–5000 or (800) 942–2677; or visit the website *www.americorps.org* or *www.nationalservice.org.*

IF YOU CAN DO MORE: Recruit a friend to join you in serving your community.

YOU'RE NEVER TOO OLD

Nearly half a million Americans age fifty-five and older share their time and talents to help solve local problems by working with the Senior Corps. For more information about the programs, contact the Corporation for National Service at *www.nationalservice.com* or visit the website *www.seniorcorps.com.* Senior Corps includes three national programs: Foster Grandparent Program, which links senior volunteers with children who need help; Senior Companion Program, which places volunteers with adults who need extra assistance; and Retired and Senior Volunteers Program (RSVP), a program that offers a wide range of service opportunities.

---

*"There are few successful adults who were not
at first successful children."*

—ALEXANDER CHASE, *PERSPECTIVES*

48 Sponsor a Child

Sponsor a child, change a life. There are tens of thousands of children worldwide in various child welfare organizations waiting for sponsors. Sponsoring a child doesn't take much time—just a few minutes to write out a small check each month. But it'll make a big difference in the life of the child you'll be sponsoring!

With most programs, you sign on to sponsor an individual child in a needy family in the United States or developing country. You are given a photograph of the child and periodic updates about your child's progress and development. Most programs focus on providing basic assistance, including education, food, clothing, shelter, and health care.

PARENTING TIP
Remember
to keep things in
perspective.

Before agreeing to sponsor a child, review several of the sponsorship charities available. Each has a slightly different approach to service. Some programs are faith-based; others are nonsectarian. Some work in the United States; others serve only overseas.

While each program has a different monthly fee (most are about $20 to $24), any contribution is appreciated. If the monthly sponsorship fees are too much for your budget, consider joining with family or friends to share the cost. Most children participate in sponsorship programs for five or six years, at the end of which you can sponsor a different child, if you wish.

There are dozens of child sponsorship organizations. The following is a list of a few leading groups:

- **Childreach:** Childreach is a global organization dedicated to making the lives of our world's children better. Founded in 1937 as the Foster Parents Plan, the worldwide PLAN International Family is made up of fourteen member organizations that are responsible for recruiting new sponsors. For more information, contact Childreach, U.S. member of PLAN International, 155 Plan Way, Warwick, RI 02886–1099; call (401) 738–5600; or visit the website *www.childreach.com.*
- **Children International:** A nonprofit humanitarian organization established in 1936, Children International helps children around the world overcome the burdens of poverty. Children International's worldwide programs benefit more than 260,000 children and their families in nineteen locations. For more information, contact Children International, P.O. Box 219055, Kansas City, MO 64121; call (800) 888–3089; or visit the website *www.childreninternational.org.*
- **Christian Children's Fund:** The Christian Children's Fund began sixty years ago as a missionary's wish to help children devastated by war. It has evolved into a community of caring that reaches children and families all around the world. Currently, the fund assists more than 2.5 million children in more than thirty countries. The program helps needy children regardless of race, gender, or religion. To donate or to find out how to sponsor a child, contact Christian Children's Fund, 2821 Emerywood Parkway, Box 26484, Richmond, VA 23261–5066; call (800) 776–6767; or visit the website *www.christianchildrensfund.org.*
- **Feed the Children:** Founded in 1979 by Larry Jones, Feed the Children is dedicated to providing for the needs of children, families, and persons in need in

the United States and internationally. Feed the Children distributes millions of pounds of food directly to the needy in all fifty states. The food is provided free of cost to recipients. Feed the Children's international outreach program includes feeding the hungry, development, and self-help, as well as medical and emergency assistance to needy children in eighty-five countries. For more information, contact Feed the Children, 333 North Meridian Avenue, Oklahoma City, OK 73107–6568; call (405) 942–0228; or visit the website *www.feedthechildren.org.*

- **Save the Children:** Both in the United States and around the world, Save the Children provides a safety net for needy children. The organization was formed in 1932 to respond to the needs of children in Appalachia. The mission spread to European children during World War II and now reaches worldwide. For more information, contact Save the Children, 54 Wilton Road, Westport, CT 06880; call (800) 728–3843; or visit the website *www.savethechildren.org.*

IF YOU CAN DO MORE: Consider getting a group of friends or coworkers to sponsor a club or group to sponsor children. In addition to your monthly contributions, you could work together to prepare care packages or special gifts to "your" children, if the program you are working with accepts individual donations.

℘ WORDS OF WISDOM ℘

"In nothing do we more nearly approach the Gods, than by doing good for their fellow man."

—CICERO

Become a Foster Parent

In 2000, a record 568,000 children were reported to be in foster care. About one out of every five of those children is awaiting adoption, while the others are in transition. Sometimes foster children return to their parents or another relative; other times they spend years in a state of flux. Every child needs a safe, loving place to live; every child needs to be a part of a family.

PARENTING TIP
Apologize to your children when you do something wrong.

In most states, both government and private agencies provide foster care. Potential care providers are screened and trained by sponsoring organizations. Most systems look for certain qualifications for prospective foster parents, including:

- people who are eager to provide care and supervision to children;
- people who work well with both social workers and biological parents;
- people who are able to help children develop emotionally and physically;
- people who listen well and are creative problem solvers;
- people who are financially independent of the foster care payment.

Foster children desperately need your help. Keep in mind that the task is not an easy one. Foster children in the United States are three to six times more likely than children not in care to have emotional, behavioral, and developmental problems, including conduct disorders, depression, difficulties in school, and impaired social relationships. Some experts estimate that about 30 percent of the children in care have serious emotional problems. According to a 1995 GAO study, 58 percent of young children in foster care had serious health problems and 62 percent had been subject to prenatal drug exposure, placing them at risk of other health problems. Of former foster care children, 66 percent do not receive a high school diploma, 61 percent have no work experience, 34 percent go on welfare, and 25 percent end up on the streets. Daunting statistics, no doubt. But these grim numbers only underscore the critical need for loving, responsible people to take an interest in those children. Your positive influence as a foster parent can mitigate some of the challenges faced by these children.

If you are interested in becoming a foster parent, contact your state's foster care specialist. Contact the Children's Bureau, Department of Health and Human Services, 330 Independence Avenue, S.W., Washington, DC 20201; call (202) 619–0257; or visit the website *www.acf.dhhs.gov/programs/cb/parent/fostersp.htm*. You can also learn more about foster care by visiting the website *www.fostercare.org*; this site includes links to foster care specialists and resources in every state.

> **IF YOU CAN DO MORE:** Make a commitment to work with more than one child. You may want to work with several siblings at one time or to continue as a foster parent after your children move on to another arrangement.

❧ WORDS OF WISDOM ❧

"There never was a person who did anything worth doing who did not receive more than he gave."
—HENRY WARD BEECHER

PROFILES IN NUMBERS

The following information was collected by the Adoption and Foster Care Analysis and Reporting System of the U.S. Department of Health and Human Services, Children's Bureau.

How old are children in foster care?

Less than 1	4%
1 to 5 years	25%
6 to 10 years	26%
11 to 15 years	28%
16 to 18 years	16%
Over 18	2%

How long do children stay in foster care?

Less than 1 month	3%
1 to 5 months	16%
6 to 11 months	14%
12 to 17 months	11%
18 to 23 months	9%
24 to 29 months	8%
30 to 35 months	6%
3 to 4 years	15%
5 years or more	18%

When children are adopted out of foster care, what is the relationship of adoptive parents to the child prior to adoption?

Non-relative	20%
Foster parent	64%
Other relative	16%

Adopt a Child

A really BIG way to help children and to share your love is to adopt a child. Hundreds of thousands of children in the United States and abroad wait for loving homes, for parents who'll care for them and give them a sense of belonging.

PARENTING TIP

Learn what your children have to teach you.

The adoption process differs, depending on whether you work with a state agency, a private adoption agency, or the birth parents and their representatives.

• **Public adoptions:** Children in the public child welfare system are placed for adoption by public, government-operated agencies or by private agencies under contract with the government.

• **Private agency adoptions**: In private agency adoptions, children are placed in non-relative homes by nonprofit or for-profit agencies licensed by the state.

• **Independent adoptions:** In independent or non-agency adoptions, children are placed in non-relative homes directly by the birth parents or through services of a doctor, attorney, or member of the clergy.

Domestic Adoption

Most laws involving adoption are enacted at the state level. They can be quite complex, so try to become familiar with the laws of your state as you explore the adoption option. If you're interested in becoming an adoptive parent through the state, contact your state's adoption specialist.

Contact the Children's Bureau, Department of Health and Human Services, 330 Independence Avenue, S.W., Washington, DC 20201; call (202) 619–0257; or visit the website *www.acf.dhhs.gov/programs/cb.htm*.

For more information about adoption, contact the National Adoption Information Clearinghouse, 330 C Street, S.W., Washington, DC 20447; call (703) 352–3488 or (888) 251–0075; or visit the website *www.calib.com/naic/ parents/index.htm*.

MAKING ADOPTION AFFORDABLE

Most private adoption agencies charge fees to help defray the costs of adoption services. More than seventy companies nationwide offer adoption benefits to their employees to help defray adoption expenses, including court costs and legal fees. For more information, contact the National Adoption Center, 1500 Walnut Street, Suite 701, Philadelphia, PA 19102; call (215) 735–9988 or (800) TO ADOPT; or visit the website *www.nac.adopt.org/nac/nac.html*.

An additional source of information on financial resources for adoption is offered by the National Endowment for Financial Education. The web page "How to Make Adoption an Affordable Option" can be found at *www.nefe.org/adoption/defalt.htm*.

International Adoption

International adoption is an excellent option for many families, especially those who want to adopt an infant. The process can be complex and expensive, however, depending on the country from which you adopt. Costs and waiting time vary significantly, depending on the age of the child you want to adopt. Costs for foreign adoption can range from $12,000 to $30,000, but most adoptions run in the $15,000 to $20,000 range. The waiting time for international adoption, including the home study and Immigration and Naturalization Services approval process, can take from one to three years.

To become familiar with the process of international adoption, visit the U.S. Department of State, Office of Children's Issues, at *http://travel.state.gove/adopt.html*. In addition, the National Adoption Information Clearing-house provides resources on international adoption; visit the website *www.calib.com/naic/parents/index.htm*.

IF YOU CAN DO MORE: Adopt another child!

SPECIAL CHILDREN, SPECIAL PARENTS

Special-needs children can bring immeasurable joy to any family equipped to meet their needs. Usually there is no fee to adopt a child with special needs through a public agency. (If the agency does charge a fee, it is usually reimbursed once the adoption is finalized.)

The federal government provides two financial assis-tance programs for special-needs adoptions. One is a one-time reimbursement of $2,000 for adopting a special-needs child; the second is ongoing adoption assistance by the state on behalf of eligible children. For more information about financial support programs in your state, contact your state adoption specialist. You can also claim a tax credit when you adopt a child with special needs; for details on the tax consequences of adoption, contact the Internal Revenue Service at *www.irs.ustreas.gov*.

OTHER WEBSITES OF INTEREST

www.acf.dhhs.gov/programs A site providing information on foster care and adoption.

www.adoption.com This site has launched the International Adoption Resource Center and provides a wealth of information for those interested in pursuing adoption. You can also call (800) ADOPT–HERE.

www.adoptiveparents.com Find baby names, adoption laws, information about adoption risks, glossary of adoption terms, and more.

www.calib.com The National Adoption Information Clearinghouse, a great site with the latest information and statistics related to adoption and foster care.

www.familypreservation.com A great resource for adoption and foster parenting information.

ADOPTION FACTS

- There are about 3.3 people seeking adoption for every actual adoption.

- About 2 percent of never-married women aged fifteen to forty-four have ever adopted a child.

- Black and nonblack women are equally likely to seek adoption.

- Of women fifteen to forty-four, the percentage of women who had ever sought to adopt was highest among those who wanted three or more children, had experienced the death of a child or miscarriage, or were older.

- Most adoptive parents are in two-parent families and are age thirty-one to forty. A growing number of parents are aged forty-one to forty-nine. Most parents attended or completed college.

- People who adopt from public agencies tend to have lower levels of education and income than independent adopters.

ॐ *WORDS OF WISDOM* ॐ

"If you're not here to serve somebody, if there's going to be no integrity to your journey, no honor in it, then why are you here?"

—Harry Belafonte

Websites of Interest

If you're interested in children's issues, the following websites may be of interest to you:

www.aecf.org The Annie E. Casey Foundation sponsors a site that provides information and support in the area of child welfare; it includes a rank of the states on the basis of various measures of child welfare.

www.carnegie.org/starting_points/ The site provides an online version of "Starting Points: Meeting the Needs of Our Youngest Children," a report of the Carnegie Task Force on meeting the needs of young children.

www.centersofcompassion.org The World Centers of Compassion for Children is a nonprofit organization founded by Nobel peace laureate Betty Williams.

www.child.net/volunteer.htm This website from the National Children's Coalition can help match volunteers with children's programs.

www.childrenofthenight.org This organization is dedicated to rescuing American children from street prostitution.

www.childrenstable.org This organization works to provide meals to needy Florida children and their families.

www.futureofchildren.org This organization is dedicated to disseminating timely information on issues related to children's well-being.

www.hcnkids.org The Homeless Children's Network provides comprehensive mental health services to homeless children and their families.

www.homelesskids.org This organization is dedicated to helping homeless children around the world.

www.kidsnet.org This clearinghouse and information center is devoted to children's television, radio, audio, video, and multimedia.

www.netaid.org This e-action site involves issues of extreme poverty worldwide; it includes a way to search volunteer opportunities worldwide.

www.zerotothree.org This site focuses on child development issues of interest to parents of children from birth to age three; it is an excellent resource for all parents.

About the Author

Cheryl Saban is an author, television writer, producer, philanthropist, child advocate, and most important, wife and mother of four. She and her husband, Haim Saban, have been actively working for the welfare of children and the improvement of children's lives for many years. They both currently sponsor several children year-round through international programs such as Childreach and Save the Children Foundation.

As part of her philanthropic activism, Saban sits on multiple boards: United Friends of the Children/Bridges (an organization that dedicates its energies to helping foster youth), Children's Hospital Los Angeles (where she also volunteers as a "cuddler"), and Milken Community High School. Additionally, she is the executive director of the Saban Children's Foundation, which is involved in activities nationwide for the benefit of underprivileged children.

Cheryl Saban also actively supports the Adopt-a-School Foundation; the Los Angeles Rape Crisis Center, to which she donated the proceeds of her first novel, SINS OF THE MOTHER; the Los Angeles Free Clinic; the Westside Children's Center; the Fulfillment Fund; and numerous other charitable causes, mostly devoted to the welfare of children.

In addition to 50 WAYS TO SAVE OUR CHILDREN and SINS OF THE MOTHER, Saban is the author of MIRACLE CHILD, a nonfiction book on new reproductive technology, and GRIFFIN, a toddler board book series. She is currently working on her second novel, MIXED MESSAGES. Her credits also include writing scripts for multiple children's television shows, as well as co-writing and co-executive-producing *Au Pair* and *Au Pair II*, the two highest rated tele-movies in the history of the Fox Family Channel (now the ABC Family Channel).

Cheryl Saban has a bachelor's degree in psychology and is currently working on her master's. She has dedicated all the proceeds of this book to the benefit of children worldwide.